Grab
Life
by the
Bungees

Diane H. Nettles

Grab Life by the Bungees*

*And 50+ Other Ways to Find Humor, Hope, and Happiness After Your Partner Has Died

TEN
Alstroemerias
PRESS

Published by Ten Alstroemerias Press, Pittsburgh
www.dianenettles.com

GIRL FRIDAY
PRODUCTIONS'

Edited and designed by Girl Friday Productions
www.girlfridayproductions.com

Cover design: David Fassett
Project management: Sara Spees Addicott
Editorial production: Janice Lee
Image credits: cover © Adobe Stock/pixelrobot, Adobe Stock/Linda

ISBN (paperback): 979-8-9889755-0-2
ISBN (ebook): 979-8-9889755-1-9

Library of Congress Control Number: 2023920142

First edition

Contents

Introduction 1

Chapter 1: So Now You're a WWPD
How to Make Peace with a New Identity 13

Chapter 2: What's So Funny About Loss?
How to Build Positive Habits into Each Day 22

Chapter 3: Excuse Me, What Did You Just Say?
How to Deal with Insensitive Remarks 35

Chapter 4: ~~Happy~~ Holidays!
How to Cope with Celebrations 42

Chapter 5: I Don't Wanna!
How to Get Your Affairs in Order 56

Chapter 6: Oh No, I'm Having a Moment!
How to Handle Grief Triggers 68

Chapter 7: A Widow Walks into a Bar
How to Step Out into the World Socially 78

Chapter 8: Is This an Episode of *The Office*?
How to Guard Yourself When Going Back to Work . . 99

Chapter 9: Did Cupid Just Shoot Me?
How to Be Open to Finding Love Again 112

Chapter 10: Grabbing Life by the Bungees
How to Stay Present During Good Times 126

Chapter 11: What's the Ripple?
How to Advance Your Partner's Legacy 134

Epilogue 143

Acknowledgments 145

References 149

About the Author 157

Introduction

You may have been "prepared," knowing that your partner's death was imminent. Or maybe the death of your partner was sudden and unexpected.

Regardless of how or when it happened, that moment changed your life forever, leaving you with a tsunami of grief, and a whole bunch of things to figure out. I'm truly sorry about that. Everything about your life transformed completely, and that's a difficult thing to adjust to. And the days ahead of you will have challenging moments, too. To put it bluntly, that sucks.

The good news is that you do, indeed, have days ahead of you. (Yes, I promise—that is, indeed, good news.)

It's hard to fathom that good news right away. "Cheer up!" is an easy thing to say and nearly impossible to do when a cataclysmic shift in your life has occurred without your consent.

But who wants to be suffering from constant pain?

In *Resilient Grieving: Finding Strength and Embracing Life After a Loss That Changes Everything* (2017), Lucy Hone, who lost her twelve-year-old daughter in an automobile accident, explains that, even though she and her family had no choice in accepting her daughter's death, she contends that they did have choices in how they grieved. She states, "Exerting intentional control over our thoughts and actions helped us weather those terrible first six months" (p. 12).

And I'm willing to bet that it's been hard for you to find reasons to smile ever since.

Are you ready to read a book about smiling while you grieve the loss of your life partner? Trust me, I get it if you think the answer to that question is a definite NO. But hang in there with me. Please. It might help.

First, let me share my story.

MY WIDOW MOMENT

One February evening in 2018, my husband, Tim, and I had finally finished packing our suitcases. The next day we would be flying to an island in the Caribbean, and we were exhausted but excited. We had just settled into bed and were winding down in front of the TV, when, shortly after midnight, Tim sat up suddenly, fell over, and went perfectly still. He was sixty-one, and we had been married for thirty-eight and a half years.

The next few hours are still a blur in my mind, but I remember a few raw details.

I called 911, but with the severe hearing loss I've had all my life, the conversation with the dispatcher was a struggle. This was in the days before I had Bluetooth connections for my hearing aids. Tim was the one who made all our phone calls. Unfortunately, he was in no condition to make this call.

The dispatcher asked question after question as I strained to hear. She stuck with me, though, shouting directions on what to do. I tried reviving Tim while the responder crew was on its way.

As I sat in the front seat of the ambulance on the way to the hospital, a torrent of thoughts marched through my mind. *Do we need to postpone our trip? Is Tim going to be in the hospital for a long time? The police called Chuck, but will he know where to meet me so we can go to see his dad together? Should I call Tommy's dorm room at college? What time is it?*

Once at the hospital, Chuck and I accepted the news from the doctor on duty in stunned silence. She led us into the hospital room to see Tim. We choked out goodbyes to him as he lay on the hospital bed in a gown, with tubes in his nose, with no glasses . . . no sight . . . no life left in him.

Chuck drove me to his house, where I watched numbly as he spent the rest of the early morning hours making phone calls to his brother and grandparents. At the time, he was twenty-nine years old. He grew up a lifetime that day, February 16.

Eventually, at about 4:00 a.m., I asked Chuck to take me home. I insisted that he drop me off and then go back home to his wife; I promised I would be okay by myself.

The floor in our bedroom was littered with syringes and equipment from the emergency crew. I stepped around them and crawled into my side of the bed. I stared at the empty space on the other side of the bed and began shaking violently.

I just couldn't stop shaking. Then, and to this day, I agonized over the fact that I couldn't save him.

The next afternoon, I wrapped both my sons in a hug, sobbing, when we picked up Tommy at the airport. Silently we drove to the funeral home for our appointment. The place was packed with people attending a visitation for a young local woman who had died of cancer. It was difficult to navigate the crowd as we wandered through hallways, trying to find the office of the funeral consultant. Once we found her, she led us to a merchandise room, right across the hall from the viewing rooms, to select our funeral paraphernalia. I was in a daze, making decisions about how to "celebrate" my husband's life now that it had unexpectedly ended, and all the while, strangers from my township were peeking into our room and commenting about "who was next." It was surreal that I would be hosting a funeral in just a couple of days.

HOW THE EULOGY HELPED

As our plans for the funeral progressed, both my sons said they were going to speak. I decided that if they could handle it, then so could I.

Because Tim loved to tell stories to anyone who would listen, I knew I wanted to share a story in the eulogy. The first dilemma was—which one? There were just too many good ones to choose from! The second dilemma was how to tell the story without breaking Tim's number one rule about going to church: Get in and out in an hour!

Then I recalled this story: As much as Tim loved to talk and be with people, he absolutely hated public speaking. On the occasions when he had to, he worried for days about what to say and carefully prepared his notes on index cards. One day, several years ago, we were in the car on the way to a company function. He was the boss; he had to give a little talk to the employees and felt that he had to speak well and eloquently to them. But he had somehow left his notes at home, and there was no time to turn back and get them. So, after scrambling around in my purse for scraps of paper to write on, I proceeded to transcribe his dictation. He was frantic over re-creating his speech just right, even telling *me*, a teacher and writer, where to put the commas!

But then I realized what all the fuss was about. His overwhelming concern was not about getting the speech perfect, but about making sure to thank *everyone*. He didn't want to leave anyone out, and he didn't want anyone to feel as if they were not appreciated. This was true at work and everywhere else, for that matter.

So in my eulogy I wrote what he would want me to say to the people who came to support us on this occasion that none of us wanted to attend: *Thank you.*

I closed with one more story: Once, when Tim and I were

sitting at the bar at our favorite restaurant, having dinner, the topic of funerals came up. And he said, "I want to make one thing perfectly clear: When it's my time to go, I *do not* want a funeral."

Then I told the packed sanctuary of people at my husband's funeral, which I was *not* supposed to have, "As many of you know, marriage is a fifty/fifty endeavor. So I followed his advice about half the time."

The relief that I felt as I heard their laughter enveloped me like a shroud. These people remembered Tim fondly. Those who knew him well could probably hear him chuckle and see his eye roll at my loving jab.

And, for just a brief moment, I felt no pain.

WHY I WROTE THIS BOOK

I'm not a psychologist or therapist; I am a teacher, and I know the power of stories. Good stories teach. They speak truths. And they can also heal. This book tells my story, but it's more than that. This book is about acknowledging your story.

You may be seeking ways to help you cope with your situation. Through many years of research, my own experience, and the experiences of those I interviewed for this book, I've collected some practical ways to put some positivity and humor into the many challenges you'll face as a woman whose partner died.

Why is *positivity* important? "Positivity" is defined as "the quality of having a positive attitude" by the *Cambridge Dictionary* (n.d.). Thus, is it a personality trait? Something you're born with?

However, when you Google it, you'll find that the word "positivity" is also defined as "the practice of being or tendency to be positive or optimistic in attitude" (Oxford Languages, n.d.). This second definition indicates that having a positive attitude is a *practice*. So perhaps the quality of having a positive attitude requires a conscious, repeated effort. Perhaps such practice helps you get better at it over time.

Research tells us that training people to focus on positive things rather than negative can improve their well-being (MacLeod et al., 2002; Wadlinger & Isaacowitz, 2008). What do positive people do? They look for the bright side of difficult situations, acknowledging negativity but realizing it is not permanent (Smith, 2021). They laugh often and experience less stress (Zander-Schellenberg et al., 2020).

Psychologist (and comedian!) Brian King (2016) explains that laughter reduces stress because it reduces cortisol production in our bodies. Cortisol is the hormone released when we experience stress or trauma. Too much cortisol in the body can produce all kinds of awful things, such as high blood pressure, anxiety, depression, weight gain, sleeplessness, and headaches. But laughter, King explains, calms us.

Barbara Frederickson (2009) describes ten forms of positivity born of her research: joy, gratitude, serenity, interest, hope, pride, amusement, inspiration, awe, and love. She says, "Positivity, we've discovered, is at the heart of human resilience" (p. 99).

The science of positivity offers tremendous help during the difficult days, months, and years after losing your life partner.

But . . .

Is there such a thing as *too much* positivity? Yes. Taking positivity to an extreme is not good; it's toxic to your well-being. In fact, that's what's called "toxic positivity," and it happens when people deny, avoid, or suppress negative emotions. For example, suppose you tell a friend that your twenty-fifth anniversary is coming up and you're feeling sad because your late husband is not here to celebrate it with you. Your friend says, "Well, look on the bright side. You had twenty-five good years with your husband." While this positive statement is true, it's not going to make you feel better because it's denying how you feel about your loss. Such denial invalidates your grief. Sometimes you need to simply be with your negative feelings. You need your friend to witness your pain. Whether someone flings toxic positivity at you or you do it to yourself, it's not healthy, and it's not what I'm advocating in this book.

We all know how a good cry helps. So sit with your pain as you need to. When you're ready to shed it and feel better again, pull out the tricks of the positivity trade. Give yourself permission to enjoy a good laugh, if that makes you feel better. Madan Kataria, author of *Laughter Yoga* (2018), says that we are in control of our own joy and must be proactive about bringing more laughter into our lives. He says, "If you choose to be sad, nobody can stop you; if you choose to laugh, no one can stop that either" (p. 219).

The strategies I offer in this book helped me and continue to help me to this day, more than five years later. While I don't think the death of my life partner is one bit funny, I do believe that I can choose to make my life better by smiling and laughing—and sometimes I can do that even when I don't feel like it. I'm determined not to be stuck in sadness—my life is better than that. *Your* life is better than that.

I should add that, while I consider myself a spiritual person, I do not offer faith-based insights. There are many excellent books available on relying on faith to cope with grief; I encourage you to check them out, because they may help you tremendously. I'm all for getting whatever help you can grasp, in any form, fashion, flavor, or denomination.

Additionally, I wrote this book specifically for women who have lost a partner, because I've noticed that widows have unique challenges in facing life alone. However, the lessons I learned about positivity and humor in the face of the pain of grief can apply to anyone dealing with the loss of someone they love.

IS THIS BOOK FOR YOU?

Grief after a profound loss is a complex, multifaceted, con-
fusing beast. It affects everyone differently and can linger for
varying and surprising amounts of time. Given its wild nature
and unique impact, you may be at a place in your grief journey
where the strategies in this book aren't accessible to you. I contend you are ready to take in the lessons herein if

- you're able to handle basic functions of day-to-
  day life and are not staying in bed most of the day
  (even though sometimes you might want to);
- you're looking for ways to make your life more
  pleasant, even though you're still grieving (and
  always will grieve what you've lost);
- you want to take action to improve your life;
- you feel the pain of grief but you also want to
  feel joy;
- you want to resist dwelling on the past;
- you want to stop dreading the future; and
- you like to smile and are looking for ways to add
  smiles to your days.

Please note that if you are struggling to make it through
each day and your grief is affecting your daily functioning,
you may benefit from speaking to a grief counselor or mental
health professional. This book is not a substitute for therapy,
though it is designed to offer light healing to those who are
able to make small commitments to receiving it.

THINGS YOU'LL DISCOVER IN THIS BOOK

There are eleven short chapters in this book. In each, I've shared a personal story about the theme of that chapter, along with some strategies that helped me manage grief and cope with the mess that it creates. All the strategies are taken from practices recommended by research in humor and positivity, but I am a firm believer that not all strategies work for everybody, because of the very personal nature of grief. Depending on where you are in this journey, you may want to skip around in the book and read the chapters that are most pertinent to your life right now.

In Chapter 1, titled "So Now You're a WWPD," I explain what a WWPD is and how this acronym came to be. You'll learn about how the ugly "w" word—"widow"—affects us and changes us. I explain how you can step into your new role with dignity and feel that shift in attitude that you get when you show the world—and yourself—that you are the one in charge.

Chapter 2, "What's So Funny About Loss?," explains the role of humor and positivity in the management of grief and how you can add some lightness and joy to each day. I suggest that you think of the strategies in this chapter as "preventative medicine" so that you can make your life stronger and prepare yourself for the bumpy ride that grief brings you.

Since your partner died, have you noticed how people say really dumb things? And have you thought to yourself, *Excuse me, what did you just say?* That's the title of Chapter 3, where you'll learn about dealing with these comments and how to make yourself stronger in the process.

Holidays and special occasions can be awful. That's why I titled Chapter 4 "~~Happy~~ Holidays!" But I make some suggestions for coping with holidays and special occasions that are suddenly not so happy anymore.

In Chapter 5, "I Don't Wanna!," I discuss the drudgery of dealing with all that practical stuff that comes with your partner's death—everything from obtaining death certificates to fixing leaky pipes.

Anyone who has lost a partner knows about triggers. Those awful, pain-racked moments come out of nowhere simply because you see, smell, feel, or hear something that reminds you of who and what you've lost. Chapter 6, "Oh No, I'm Having a Moment!," gives you a few positive ways to meet triggers head-on and get through them.

Chapter 7, "A Widow Walks into a Bar," takes you on that journey of discovering how to be social again. More importantly, it shows you the importance of learning to love being with yourself—all by yourself—so that you might be alone, but not lonely.

"Is This an Episode of *The Office*?" is Chapter 8, where I describe what going back to work (if you choose to do so) can be like when you're grieving the death of your partner. I offer a few ways to get a handle on dealing with well-meaning but clueless coworkers, as well as those moments when grief takes over while you're trying to take care of business.

One of the trickiest parts of losing your partner is figuring out how to move aside and let another partner into your life—if you choose to do so. I discuss that very loaded issue in Chapter 9, "Did Cupid Just Shoot Me?"

In Chapter 10, "Grabbing Life by the Bungees," I tell the story of how I learned about "living in the moment" from my granddaughter as she rode on a bungee trampoline ride at a local festival. I offer some tips on staying with those good times, when you get them.

The book ends with Chapter 11, "What's the Ripple?" Everybody wants to matter, even after death. And it's painful to realize that this old world just spins right along after your partner dies, and people can easily forget about them. This chapter explains how there are ways to keep the memory of your partner alive, creating a ripple effect that will last.

IT GETS BETTER

You've lost your life partner. I'm so sorry.

Recently, a friend of mine lost her husband. She asked me, through her tears, "Does it ever get better?"

I promised her, as I promise you—it does get better. Eventually, you figure out how to live with this dramatic shift in your life and manage the pain it brings to you.

Robert Fulghum, author of *All I Really Need to Know I Learned in Kindergarten* (2003), said, "Laughter is the only cure for grief." Brian King, in *The Laughing Cure* (2016), wrote, "The operative term is 'help.' Laughter isn't a cure for anything, but it sure can help a lot" (pp. 70–71). This much I know: Laughter can make you feel better. I hope this book helps you discover (or rediscover) a belief in the soothing balm of a good laugh, especially when you don't feel like laughing. Even though grief never goes away, your ability to live with it does, indeed, get better. In spite of the fact that life dealt you a blow that could keep you down, you can, in time, "grab life by the bungees" and enjoy its ride.

CHAPTER 1

So Now You're a WWPD

How to Make Peace with a New Identity

It's crazy, the whole widow thing.

—Becky Aikman, *Saturday Night Widows: The Adventures of Six Friends Remaking Their Lives* (2013)

How do you like being called a "widow"?

What was your reaction the first time you had to check the "widow" box on a form?

I've known many women who have lost a spouse or life partner. And every single one of them has told me how much they despised the word "widow."

Why? What is it about that word that makes us cringe?

Does it make you feel old? Sad? Alone? Pitied by society?

Historically, widows have been considered helpless, with the need to be protected. I'll be honest: In the past, when I heard the word "widow," I thought of a woman who has no identity other than the one her spouse gave her. I wonder if that is what society now says about me. From the moment I became one, the word "widow" reminded me that I was now in a category that I wasn't ready for and didn't belong in. It made me feel old, even though the average age at which women in the United States become widows is fifty-nine—exactly the age I was when Tim died. (That's not old at all!) And we're not alone. According to the US Census Bureau American Community Survey data for 2021, widows (women whose spouses have died) make up about 9 percent of the population. There are more of us than there are widowers (men whose spouses have died), who make up a little more than 2.5 percent of the population. And a widow aged sixty or older can expect to be a widow for twelve and a half years (unless she remarries, which is not as common for women as it is for men) (Compton & Pollak, 2021).

So we are in good company.

In fact, at my husband's visitation at the funeral home, a woman who had lost her husband a few years before said to me, "Welcome to the Widow Club." (Here was an opportunity to chuckle, but frankly, I was not pleased about the new club membership, nor was I happy about her reminder of my new label.)

Google "What is the most stressful event in a person's life?" You'll see that almost every result says, "Death of a loved one." If you keep searching, you'll find the Social Readjustment Rating Scale (1967), also known as the Holmes and Rahe Stress Scale. On this scale, "death of a spouse" rates highest as a stressor that can lead to illness (p. 216). Besides being painful—emotionally, mentally, and physically—"widowing" means giving up your former identity and figuring out how to be this new person. That's extremely difficult to do, especially since it wasn't your choice.

I'm sure you've found out that there's nothing pleasant—or

funny—about becoming a widow. In this chapter, you'll learn how redefining yourself—and losing the negative connotation of the word "widow"—can help.

MY STORY: HOW I LOST MY "WIDOW" LABEL

A week after Tim died, I returned to work at the university. I was a faculty member and chairperson of the Childhood Education Department. At a university-wide faculty meeting, where all departments were represented, I introduced myself to a faculty member from another department whom I'd never met before. He said, with a nervous chuckle, "Oh, so you're the woman whose husband died!"

At first, I was a little offended about the gossip that had spread so quickly across campus. I inwardly rolled my eyes at his obvious lack of social skills. (Or maybe I wasn't so discreet—maybe I actually did roll my eyes.) I realized, with a little chuckle to myself, that sometimes even smart people aren't very smart. (Okay, maybe it wasn't a chuckle to myself— maybe I actually laughed out loud.)

But this incident gave me the opportunity to redefine myself.

I decided I could, instead of being a "widow"—a term I'd always loathed—be that "woman whose husband died." Nothing more, nothing less. It was empowering to view my- self as a woman who has been dealt a difficult situation—not as a category that is defined by society as sad, lonely, old, or helpless.

So, throughout this book, I use an acronym to refer to those of us who are classified as "widows" by the rest of the world: WWPD, or "woman whose partner died." Hello, WWPD, and thank you for being here.

HOW TO EMBRACE THE WWPD LABEL (OR NOT)

The power of redefining ourselves means that, as women whose partners died, we have control over our situation. We can grieve, but manage that grief so that it doesn't consume us or define us. We can become people who have lost the spouse and friend that we loved and still be individuals who are content with most of our life.

I learned, as I think you will, too, that humor and positivity could help me heal. I've spent much time figuring out ways to cope with the changes in my life that happened in the instant my husband died. As I met one obstacle to my happiness after another, I found one question to be one worth answering, over and over. Indeed, I have climbed out of lots of ugly and messy holes of grief by asking myself, "What would humor do to help this situation?"

So now that you are a WWPD, what are some ways to get rid of the awful connotations of widowhood? Here are some strategies you can try.

Adopt New Roles Playfully

People in our society often view a widow as broken, unable to survive without her spouse, and forever grieving. It's actually easier for many people to view widows this way, because it's hard for people to understand how a woman could be happy without her partner. We even do this to ourselves. Sometimes we believe that the amount of grief we portray "proves" how much we loved our partner.

So redefine yourself. Become a WWPD, rather than a widow to be pitied. Now that you are "alone," you've probably already learned that you must do lots of things by yourself—things that you never had to do before. For example, maybe your partner handled the family finances, and now it's up to you. Or maybe, like me, your partner did certain household chores (ugh—the laundry!), and now you are stuck with them. You've gradually had to accept these hard facts and take on new roles, whether you wanted to or not. But taking a play from the humor playbook, can you make light of these new roles? Maybe you're now the Queen of Quicken or Laundry Killer? Besides that, adding these roles to your "résumé" can help you build confidence and pride. You'll see yourself in a whole new light.

Take Control of Your Needs

Likewise, making yourself happy is something you'll need to do for yourself. No one is going to do it for you, just as no one is doing my laundry for me anymore. Accepting the responsibility for making myself happy was tough, but it was truly helpful in becoming the new person that I was going to be.

For example, shortly after Tim died, I felt the need to change the locks on the doors in my house. It may not have been logical, because my neighborhood is safe and my son and daughter-in-law live nearby. But it made me feel safer and therefore happier. So I called a locksmith and had the locks changed.

Give yourself what you need to feel safe, comforted, and happy. You're the one in charge now.

Look Inside Yourself

Try this: Name a color. Look around whatever room you're in right now, and find everything you can of that color. Make a list of those things, and continue this exercise for the rest of the day. Making note of your surroundings and choosing a focal point is a good way to train your brain to distract itself from grief and pay attention to positivity. Easy, right?

Once you get the hang of noticing things around you, turn your attention inward. What are your own characteristics—physical or personality-wise—that you admire? Appreciate the ways that you are a good friend, parent, sister, human. Notice all the things big and small your body does for you. List your traits. Reread them. Remember that you are a WWPD, but you're also so much more.

Get Rid of One Bad Thing

Do you have any habits that hold you back from making your life a more positive one? Is there something you can get rid of? Do it. This is the time of your life to make yourself feel better. And if that means you need to eliminate a habit, then now, more than ever, is the time to do it.

For example, I was accustomed to letting my husband do lots of simple things for me, such as making phone calls (I'm 85 percent deaf), fixing things around the house, and organizing files. When he died, I was lost. At first, I had lots of assistance. (In fact, my family and I laughed about the number of assistants I needed to get through the week. I even hired someone to help me organize my house and make calls for me.) But after a few months, I realized that I could not depend on others to continually fill the void caused by the loss of my husband. I had hundreds of phone calls to make. I had no choice but to make them myself. I had a twenty-five-year-old house that constantly needed repairs and updates. I could call someone to fix every tiny little thing but soon realized that the expense was ridiculous, and once the pandemic came along in 2020, getting help around the house was next to impossible.

So I lost my bad habit of dependence. I got a Bluetooth hearing aid that enabled me to make phone calls. I learned to fix a leaky faucet. I figured out how to balance a checkbook all over again. These things made me feel better about myself as I shed the label of helpless widow. Trust me, I have lots of other bad habits that I'm not quite ready to give up yet! Becoming a WWPD was traumatic enough—I don't have to change *everything* right now.

If you can just lose one "bad" habit, it might make you feel better and stronger. What can you lose?

Be a Blank Canvas

Being a WWPD forces you to be someone different from the person you were before your partner's death. This can sadden you, or it can be an opportunity for growth. Why not take the opportunity to do things you were never able to do as part of a couple? It doesn't have to involve anything extravagant.

For example, Tim loved watching TV. As soon as he walked in the door, he turned one on. Even when he left the room, he left the TV on, and there were sometimes TVs on different channels throughout the house. (I'm not a TV person, so this habit of his drove me crazy!)

When I returned to our bedroom the night he died, the TV was still on. I actually could not figure out how to use the remote and turn it off! (Like I said, I'm not a TV person.) Thus, I yanked the plug out of the wall. It remained unplugged until a year later when I removed the TV and gave it away.

Instead of the sound of various TVs wafting through the house in the evenings, I now listen to cheerful music, read, paint, or watch a comedy routine on my laptop. These things were challenging to do when Tim was around, and I found that being open to filling the silence with what I needed was absolutely vital to my well-being. It's part of the way I live now, and it helps me live with myself comfortably.

What little things can you take on now? Maybe your

partner was allergic to cats. Now you can be a cat owner. Identify at least one empty space that you can fill with something that would bring you joy.

IN THE BLINK OF AN EYE

One second, you're a wife—the next, you're a widow. That shift in your life happened instantly. The change to becoming a WWPD is a more gradual one, but it is part of who you will be for the rest of your life. There are many challenges, as you know very well. Your physical health, emotional well-being, social life, and financial security have all been affected, and sometimes it's not been a good change. When I came up for air, about a year after Tim died, and came out of my "widow's fog" season, I realized that it was up to me, and no one else, to make my life into whatever it was going to be. I figured, well, it might as well be a good one—a life that includes laughter again. I hope yours can be, too. You've survived a traumatic experience, and it takes a lot of self-care to get back on track. I hope you can find reasons to genuinely smile again.

RESOURCES THAT HELPED ME REDEFINE MY IDENTITY

Aikman, B. (2013). *Saturday night widows: The adventures of six friends remaking their lives.* New York: Broadway Books.

> *This engaging book is a memoir—the story of six widows who joined together in a support group of their own, after finding that many such groups didn't meet their needs. The writer's tone is delightfully honest and humorous. I recommend this memoir for any widow who wants to be uplifted and feel vindicated about* not *seeking therapy.*

St-Germain, K. (2023). *The widowed mom podcast.* Available from https://www.coachingwithkrista.com/podcastlaunch/

Krista St-Germain is a life coach who specializes in working with widows. She has a gentle, uplifting approach to helping widowed moms live with and manage grief.

CHAPTER 2

What's So Funny About Loss?

How to Build Positive Habits into Each Day

I wish I could tell you that laughter would solve so many of our problems, but it won't and it doesn't. What it does do is make life better.

—Brian King, *The Laughing Cure: Emotional and Physical Healing—A Comedian Reveals Why Laughter Really Is the Best Medicine* (2016)

Now that you are a WWPD, do you find that smiling is difficult?

Do you look in the mirror and see someone different from the one you were before your partner died? (Maybe one with more frown lines than you'd like?)

Does grief take over your days?

Is it impossible to be strong right now?

Does the mere thought of laughing make you want to scream?

Maybe your answer to all those questions is yes. Hey, I've been there. At times, I've felt like it was impossible to see the positive side of my situation, and in fact, if I'm in the throes of grief, I don't want anyone trying to point that out to me.

So if that's where you are right now, you can skip this chapter for a little while. I understand completely and have been in that spot before. But promise me that you will pick this back up and read it when you're ready.

When you're grieving, is there a funny side to *anything*? My answer to that question is also yes.

You've probably heard or read that Elisabeth Kübler-Ross formulated five stages of grieving: denial, anger, bargaining, depression, and acceptance. These stages are used frequently in grief therapy. Her book *On Grief and Grieving* (2005), co-authored with David Kessler, explains the stages, which were based on her research with people who have terminal illness. Sometimes it's assumed that people who are bereaving must progress through these stages sequentially and that once the last one, "acceptance," is reached, the period of grieving is over. However, Kübler-Ross did not intend the stages to be experienced in a lockstep manner. Moreover, anyone who has experienced the loss of a loved one knows that grieving is not a set of benchmarks, nor does grieving ever really go away.

In *Saturday Night Widows* (2013), Becky Aikman describes a visit to a psychologist, who told her that, instead of following rigid stages, people who are grieving fluctuate between feeling sad and feeling normal. She was enormously relieved, saying, "My ability to crack up with laughter in some of the darkest moments wasn't shameful—it was natural, and helpful, too" (p. 73).

Cracking up with laughter—however impossible it

seems—might be the best thing you can do for yourself right now. According to Allen Klein in *The Healing Power of Humor* (1989), calling on humor in difficult times "gives us perspective and keeps us in balance when life seems out of balance" (p. 165). It can help us become stronger, wiser, and more resilient. I'm a firm believer that, as Scott Weems says in *Ha!* (2014), his book on laughter, "without the ability to laugh, we wouldn't have a way to react to much that happens to us" (p. 184).

George Bonanno, in *The Other Side of Sadness* (2019), tells us about some research that he and Dacher Keltner did on the mental health of widows and widowers. Their study indicated that "people who showed genuine smiling or laughter when they talked about their loss coped better over time" (p. 58).

I invite you to know this: It's possible to feel something other than pain while you grieve. I want to show you that while the pain of grieving is natural and necessary, it can be managed, just as pain born of any misfortune can be. It's possible, and even necessary, to manage your grief with positive habits.

You can find those times when you can smile right through your grief. You can feel something other than pain while you grieve. So think of this chapter as a guide for using laughter as preventative medicine; the strategies offered here can help you improve your overall outlook and feel lighter as you move through your days. Just as you use exercise and a balanced diet to stay physically well, you can use positivity to stay well between the ears. Give some of the strategies in this chapter a try.

MY STORY: FINDING A REASON TO SMILE

My friend Ginny came to the house as soon as I called to tell her that Tim had died. She simply sat there with me. I honestly don't remember much about what she did or said. I just remember that she was there. She didn't ask, "How can I help?"

(and I was too numb to answer that anyway). She just showed up on the worst morning of my life.

Several weeks later, she and I were talking about that fateful morning. She said, "When I got to your house that morning, you were doing laundry. Why?" I really didn't know the answer. The only thing I could think of was this: Tim did all our laundry, because he didn't like the way I did it. So, early in our marriage, I was happy to let him take over the laundry room. For years, he did laundry first thing every morning. The morning he died, I figured it was now my turn again. Ginny and I got a good chuckle out of that.

There was nothing funny about what I experienced that early morning of February 16. I certainly didn't feel like laughing anytime I recalled it. But in that conversation with my friend, I was given a brief respite in my grief. Ginny and I saw a tiny bit of humor in the situation, and for just a minute I could laugh.

Another friend of mine, Kathy, was out of town the day my husband died. She got the news and flew home immediately. When her flight landed, she called me and said, "Will you be home at 10:00 this morning? I'm coming over with a notepad. I'll check your refrigerator and make a grocery list of things you might need. And don't worry about meals for the next week. I've got that covered. All I need from you is an approximate head count of people who will be around to help you these next few days." And that's what she did. I didn't have to think or answer questions about how she could help.

About three days after the funeral, when I still had several hungry out-of-town family members at the house, one of the women with whom Kathy had coordinated to provide food dropped off some breakfast items. They appeared to be delicious from their packaging. Only problem was they were frozen rock-solid, with no directions on how to cook or assemble. No one had the energy or time to thaw the food and then figure out the directions. So we consumed toast and coffee instead, and joked about how my husband would get a kick out of this situation.

I'll always be grateful to Ginny and Kathy for getting me through a very difficult time. They didn't ask, "What do you need?" They just showed up and did it. And they shared some laughs with me, giving me a few moments of relief from the pain.

Those are the kinds of moments that make a grieving heart stronger. I contend that you can only take so much pain. You need moments of respite. You need tiny little pieces of joy even in the midst of pain.

HOW TO INFUSE POSITIVITY INTO DAILY LIVING

The great thing about humor is that it helps us change perspective and shift our thinking, if only momentarily, from the ever-present pain and numbness that grief brings. As Melissa Mork says in her book, *Navigating Grief with Humor* (2019), "Is it okay to grieve with humor? Oh, my friend, it is imperative" (p. 129).

Here are some suggestions for ways to strengthen yourself with a bit of laughter and positivity—your preventative medicine—through those mind-boggling days of grief.

Read Positively

If you are a reader (or even if you're not), try adding positivity to your library. You won't always feel like reading, and you may find that your interests change drastically or that suddenly you don't feel like reading much at all for a while after your partner has died. You might have received books from well-meaning friends and found that some were helpful but others weren't.

Grief is a highly personal experience, so seek out reading

material that appeals to you, and don't feel guilty about staying away from reading material that depresses you. Shown here is a list of some books that might successfully divert your attention when you need distraction from your grieving. Some of them are thought-provoking and helpful. Many of these authors are just plain hilarious, and some have even written about losing a partner with a dash of humor.

The First Phone Call from Heaven by Mitch Albom
The Time Keeper by Mitch Albom
Dave Barry's Book of Bad Songs by Dave Barry
Bossypants by Tina Fey
Dad Is Fat by Jim Gaffigan
The Obstacle Is the Way: The Timeless Art of Turning Trials into Triumph by Ryan Holiday
Dead People Suck by Laurie Kilmartin
Make 'Em Laugh by Debbie Reynolds and Dorian Hannaway
The Way I Heard It by Mike Rowe
The End of Your Life Book Club by Will Schwalbe
You Are a Badass: How to Stop Doubting Your Greatness and Start Living an Awesome Life by Jen Sincero
Black Widow: A Sad-Funny Journey Through Grief for People Who Normally Avoid Books with Words Like "Journey" in the Title by Leslie Gray Streeter
Confessions of a Mediocre Widow: Or, How I Lost My Husband and My Sanity by Catherine Tidd
Betty White: In Person by Betty White

I've found that this positive-reading habit works almost like taking a daily vitamin. It just feels good to laugh, and the effect lingers even after I close the book.

Put a Chuckle in the Mail

Who do you know that could use a good laugh? Send them something to smile about—comics, photographs, memes, stories, or jokes—anything funny works. The key here is to send the funny stuff to someone else, because the act of stepping outside yourself, thinking of someone else, and making them laugh is more powerful than keeping it to yourself. You might even make it a new way to start each day.

For example, sometimes I can't think of my own cheery stuff, so I turn to those who make people laugh for a living. I am one of the few people left on this planet who still subscribes to a printed newspaper. Weekly, I read the comics and cut out or take a photo of my favorites. I like to send these funnies to my good friends and family. (If you don't subscribe to a paper, seek out funny memes or jokes online. Daily humor quotes are fun to look up, too.) Commit yourself to this: Every day share something that makes someone smile. At the very least, smile at someone else, even if for no reason at all.

You may be surprised at how good it feels to send funny thoughts to other people.

Stop That Chattering

In his book titled *Chatter: The Voice in Our Head, Why It Matters, and How to Harness It* (2021), psychologist Ethan Kross describes "chatter" as the inner voice that each of us has. We spend much time listening to that voice, but it's mostly negative thoughts that we attend to, because the human brain is wired to pay attention to threats to its well-being. Kross explains how to quiet the negative voice that is so terribly influential. One of the steps he suggests is to use "distanced self-talk," by using your name and addressing yourself in third person. For example, when I feel negativity kick in, I say, "Diane, you are powerful. So get going! You can do that awful thing that you dread. Remember, the worst has already happened."

Picturing myself as a superwoman in a cape, tackling a challenge for the day, helps. At the very least, I can laugh at myself as I think of myself wearing a brightly colored unitard.

So give it a try. Find good, strong, positive places to put your mind. Silence the negative inner voice with your own super-woman self-talk.

Just Smile, Dammit!

Tim was the photographer in our family. When our sons were young, he took pictures of every vacation, every family event—well, just about everything. Whenever Tim announced that it was time for a photo, we reluctantly lined up for it. More than once, our boys heard from their father, "Okay, everybody, look at me. And smile, dammit!"

So hear me out. Try it. Every morning, just stand in front of the mirror and smile. Give yourself a big grin, even if you don't feel like smiling (and perhaps *especially* if you don't feel like smiling). You may be surprised at how much better it makes you feel to see your own smile looking back at you.

In *The Laughing Cure* (2016), Brian King explains the James-Lange theory of psychology, which is the idea that the human body informs the brain about its emotion, and the act of smiling actually triggers our brains to make us feel good, rather than the other way around. In other words, "we aren't laughing because we are happy, we're happy because we're laughing. . . . Smiling and laughing make us happy or, to state it more scientifically, increase our experience of positive affect" (p. 6).

I tried this trick as a daily ritual, first thing every morning. I did a couple of armband stretches in front of the mirror and forced myself to smile while doing so. Five years later, I've kept this routine and am surprised at how much better I feel after two minutes of stretching with a smile. At the very least, I'm getting some exercise done.

Thus, if you want to make yourself feel better, just smile, dammit!

Meet One Tiny Little Goal at a Time

Focus on work to be done, tasks to be completed, and goals to be reached. Give yourself a small goal to reach daily. At the beginning, you might find your goals to be very fundamental, and that's okay. When my life was nothing but a fog, I made goals such as "Brush your teeth. Wear matching shoes." In fact, I often laughed at myself for having such mundane goals, because before becoming a WWPD, I had many lofty and complicated goals—that I actually met.

You may be feeling as if you're "not doing anything." But you are. Recognize that your brain has experienced some major trauma, so you'll need to be gentle with it. And since every day your motivation and emotions might be different, set an intention when you wake up. It might be as simple as "Check email." The point is to make a commitment and strive to meet it. Having a simple focus with a definitive outcome can be enormously helpful as you grapple with getting through the day. And once you get through one day, meeting all those little goals, you can get through another one tomorrow.

Be Nice to the Most Important Person: You!

When she found out my husband had died, my doctor (who is also a friend) gave me this advice: "Do something nice for yourself every day." What a simple yet life-altering mantra that was for me! That tiny little piece of advice still helps me tremendously. Each day during that first year after Tim died, I literally forced myself to do at least one thing I enjoyed.

What can you do to be nice to yourself? What worked for me was having a comfortable pair of slippers waiting for me when I got home from work. (Mine have smiley faces on them, thanks to my sister, who gave them to me, and they literally make me smile every time I put them on.) Whatever made you smile before your partner died can still make you smile. What are some things you can do to be nice to yourself? Think about these daily "be nice to yourself" possibilities:

- Listen to a favorite song.
- Wear a favorite T-shirt.
- Put a flower or two on your desk or table.
- Buy a new houseplant (or water the ones you already have!).
- Buy a new fragrant hand lotion.
- Use some essential oils to fill a room with fragrance.
- Watch a how-to YouTube video on something you want to learn how to do.
- Watch a cute puppy or kitten video.
- Do a puzzle—crossword, Sudoku, or word search.
- Savor a cup of coffee or tea.
- Use the fine china or crystal.

Record Three (Okay, Maybe Only One or Two) Funny Things a Day

At the end of the day, write down three funny things that happened to you that day. (If you can't think of three funny things, write down one funny thing. Or write down something that is positive—heck, just write *anything* positive, anything at all!) If you don't feel like writing, try making a habit of telling these things to a friend or family member. Or just remind yourself of something funny that happened that day. This type of "laughter intervention" is a simple way to end the day on a positive note.

Give Yourself a Laughter Permit

Grief will always be part of your life. (If you don't already know that, I'm sorry to break that to you, but it's true.) So counter-attack with laughter, as much as you can. It's been said, in hundreds of places, that "laughter is the best medicine." Robert Provine, who was a psychologist, a professor, a leading expert on laughter, and an author of two books and numerous articles, concluded that there's still a lot to be learned about the "science" of laughter, but we do know that it brings people together and it's simply enjoyable (2000).

Tickling your funny bone doesn't mean that you're "over" your loss. Your grief will still be there. But go ahead and make a vow to read or watch something funny every day. When you are proactive about it, setting aside a few minutes every day, you're training your body and mind in the habit of relaxing and being cheered up. You'll begin to look forward to it. And in moments when grief strikes hard with triggers that blindside you (see Chapter 6), it will be much easier to allow yourself this break from sadness, because your soul is already primed to expect it.

Heck, you can even tell jokes. Make jokes about your dead partner, if you wish. Sometimes those jokes are the best ones.

DANCING ALONE MAY NOT BE FUNNY, BUT IT'S A GOOD HABIT!

I've always liked to dance, even though I'm not very good at it. Let's just say that I can move quickly while music is playing—and my moves do not necessarily match the beat. I might add that Tim was even worse than I was. (We once tried ballroom dancing lessons and were asked to leave. But that didn't stop us from getting out on the dance floor whenever we had the opportunity to do so at weddings, parties, and other such events.)

About three months after Tim died, after another quiet evening alone with the TV off and eating dinner while I answered emails and graded papers, I got up from my desk to go to bed. I looked up at the urn on the mantel and wanted to cry because, at that moment, the weight of being alone fell on me. But for some reason, I was compelled to turn on some music. I searched for something upbeat and found "Kokomo" by the Beach Boys.

And I danced, in my living room, by myself.

It felt wonderful—it gave me a physical and emotional release. I gave Tim's urn a little pat on its lid before I went upstairs to bed.

From that night forward, for a long time, I made dancing alone a nightly ritual. Dancing didn't change my situation; I was still grieving. But it made me feel better, and for a few minutes it made me smile as I thought about the times we laughed while dancing sloppily but happily.

While there might not be a funny side to *everything*, there's strength in positivity. I hope you will look for it. It'll help you.

RESOURCES THAT HELPED ME UNDERSTAND
THE VALUE OF HUMOR IN EACH DAY

King, B. (2016). *The laughing cure: Emotional and physical healing—A comedian reveals why laughter really is the best medicine.* New York: Skyhorse Publishing.

Brian King is a comedian and psychologist who brings us a unique perspective on the importance of laughter and how to add more humor to our lives. He does not specifically focus on dealing with death; however, reading the book is an excellent way to learn more about how laughter enables us to cope with life in general. Additionally, and ironically, it's one of the few books about the subject of humor that's actually funny. It is a joy to read and truly helps to distract and manage the grieving mind, even though its purpose is not to help the WWPD cope with grief. King's book would be a wonderful addition to your library if you're interested in reading about how humor can help.

Klein, A. (1998). *The courage to laugh: Humor, hope, and healing in the face of death and dying.* New York: Jeremy P. Tarcher / Putnam.

Allen Klein provides three sections in this book (published thirty-two years ago), all of which show the reader how to use humor as a tool for coping with life's trials. Part 1 explains why laughter is important to the human experience and its scientific benefits. Part 2 provides fourteen techniques for using humor during adversity. And Part 3 addresses humor in grieving death. Klein's focus in all chapters is on the fact that humor refocuses the troubled mind. He says, "Humor lends a fresh eye. . . . When we can find some humor in our upsets, they no longer seem as large or as important as they once did. Humor expands our limited picture frame and gets us to see more than just our problem" (p. 11).

Klein's book is not focused entirely on grief; however, his suggestions for using humor to deal with life's difficulties can be extremely helpful for the WWPD.

CHAPTER 3

Excuse Me, What Did You Just Say?

How to Deal with Insensitive Remarks

He knew that you can't really be strong until you see the funny side of things.

—Ken Kesey, *One Flew Over the Cuckoo's Nest* (1962)

When you were at your partner's funeral, did people say things to you that made you sadder than you already were? Or maybe even angry?

Perhaps you've found yourself in the position of answering questions that shouldn't have been asked. Or maybe, since your partner died, people have tried to "cheer you up" with remarks that made you scratch your head in wonder at the sheer stupidity of what they said.

This chapter focuses on using humor and a positive attitude to manage your reaction to the insensitivity that surrounds death and grieving. You've probably found that remarks and attitudes don't stop once the funeral is over. It's been more than five years for me and I still grapple with things people say. I'll give you a few suggestions that have worked for me, and maybe they'll work for you, too.

MY STORY: THE STUPIDEST THING
I HEARD THAT DAY

I have always known, because we had discussed it several times, that my husband wanted to be cremated. But since Tim died suddenly and unexpectedly, I felt that it was important for our sons and his parents to see him one last time. So I had him placed in a rental casket for a private visitation. (He was the general manager of a rental car company in Pittsburgh. I thought he'd get a kick out of *renting* the casket!)

The open-casket viewing was private, for family only. Then we closed the casket and had a public visitation.

Tim was larger than life, in many ways. In the last decade of his life, he had gained weight, and while he went to the gym religiously, he also enjoyed a good thick steak and ice cream for dessert. Consequently, he was always battling those last twenty pounds.

At the public visitation, a friend of ours, who has a booming projectile voice, approached me in the receiving line. With a loud guffaw, he asked, "Wow, how did they fit Tim in that casket?"

I chuckled awkwardly and quickly found someone else to talk to.

Grief heightens one's sensitivity to almost everything. I found that many well-meaning people—like my friend in the above example—said, quite frankly, what I thought were the *stupidest* things. These things sometimes made me angry, even though I knew people meant well. They cared enough to say something, even though their word choices were not so thoughtful, or even if it was a clumsy attempt to bring humor to the situation. (Quite honestly, Tim would probably have gotten a good laugh out of the casket comment, spoken by a good friend.)

HOW TO HANDLE RIDICULOUS SYMPATHIES

Have you been subjected to comments that sting, even if they were intended to be comforting? While I'm not excusing stupidity, it might help to remember that many people in Western cultures are generally uncomfortable with death.

Thus, you will probably continue to experience nervous laughter, poor jokes, or nervously awkward hugs accompanied by stiff and perfunctory comments such as "Sorry for your loss." This awkwardness can go on for *years*.

So, how can you respond to insensitive but well-meaning remarks? Listed below are a few strategies that I used, which helped.

Say Whatever the Heck You Want to Say

I'm convinced that there's no "right" way to respond to insensitive remarks. I've heard that some WWPDs have focused on educating people to say more appropriate things to those who grieve. There are whole books written on the subject! Yet I'm convinced that there are some things you just cannot fix. So my advice is to respond in any way you want. You're the one grieving. You're excused. Say anything, or say nothing at all.

Here are a few things people have actually said to me, with my response—whether I said it aloud or kept it to myself—in parentheses:

- "I heard the news and it ruined my morning."
  (Yes, my morning was also ruined.)
- "What are you going to do in that big house all by
  yourself?" (Why do you ask?)
- "Last year we had flooding in our town, and
  now this—your husband dies. It seems as if God
  is punishing us." (I really prefer to think God
  wouldn't punish anyone with my husband's
  death.)
- "I'm sorry for your loss. And, who are you?" (Oh,
  I must've forgotten my name tag, as I stand here
  next to my husband's coffin.)
- "I was real surprised to hear your husband passed
  away. Were you surprised, too?" (Um . . . yeah.)
- "You and I are going through the same thing. My
  wife and I are getting a divorce." (I'm sorry to hear
  that, but I feel quite sure that it's not the same
  thing.)
- "So, other than dealing with your husband's passing, what have you been up to?" (Well, dealing
  with my husband's passing has taken up quite a
  bit of my time and energy.)
- "You look like you've lost weight. That's good. I
  guess that's how you deal with it, huh? You don't
  eat? Well, that's better than eating too much."
  (Um . . . thank you . . . ?)
- "I've got one up on you. All three of my husbands
  died of a heart attack. I decided to stop getting
  married." (Wow, I guess I'm a little behind . . .)
- "I'm sorry I didn't come to the funeral. I had a
  ladies' golf match that morning that I just couldn't
  miss." (Oh. Gee, thanks for sharing. I hope your
  golf match went well.)
- "Didn't you two have an argument toward the

end?" (What? What could possibly be the reason
for your question? And the answer is no.)

- "You're so strong. That's what he would want . . ."
  (Well, I'm not feeling all that strong. But if I am
  strong, it's because that's what *I* choose to do.)

Write Down That Crazy Stuff

Writing can be therapeutic. So grab a journal and write down
all the craziest lines you've heard. Seeing their words in print
can help you look at the situation a little more objectively; with
hindsight, you might even see how funny they actually were.

Shrug It Off (Sticks and Stones Can
Break My Bones, but Words . . .)

When you're grieving, things that didn't bother you before you
became a WWPD are suddenly painful. It feels as if no one in
this world understands what you're going through. People say
things that make no sense. Or they try to cheer you up with
platitudes like "Everything happens for a reason." (Makes you
just want to smack 'em, right?)

The problem is there really isn't anything good that
can be said. People often say things with a look of pity, but
being pitied is condescending. What you need is empathy,
which is comforting. But sometimes people—even the most
well-meaning friends and family—just don't know how to be
empathetic.

So, what's the worst that happens when people say stupid
things? You've made it through the death of your partner. You
can make it through the stupid things people say.

Sometimes you just gotta give grace and move away from
that negativity.

Now That You Know—Help Another WWPD

When you encounter someone who has lost their partner, keep your lessons learned in mind. Two friends of mine, whose husbands died in the last couple of years, after I became a WWPD, said, "Oh, I'm so sorry. I didn't say the right things to you after Tim died. Now I know."

Even after all you've experienced as a WWPD, you might still find it hard to know what to say to someone who grieves. But now you know. You may want to offer sincere condolences and a piece of your heart, because you've been there and you know this journey is a struggle. Thus, try to keep your remarks simple yet heartfelt. Honestly, the only thing that really needs to be said is "I'm so sorry."

TIME—AND HUMOR—HELPS

Over time, humor changes perspective. Think about the many things in your life before your partner died that weren't humorous when they happened, but became a "this will be funny in ten years" story. The same is true of insensitive and thoughtless remarks that you've had to cope with as you grieve. After a while, they don't sting as much. And sometimes, they do become genuinely funny—they might even become "this will be funny in ten years" stories.

You can choose to forgive thoughtless people. It might make you feel better. At the very least, you can choose to ignore them.

You can also choose to smile. You might find that laughter helps just as much as tears do.

RESOURCES THAT HELPED ME DEAL WITH HOW TO RESPOND TO STUPID THINGS PEOPLE SAY

Devine, M. (2017). *It's OK that you're not OK.* Boulder, CO: Sounds True.

Megan Devine is a psychotherapist who lost her partner, Matt, in a drowning accident. Her book is about her realization that grief therapy has gotten it all wrong and how our culture makes grieving even more difficult than it already is. She debunks so much of what we have heard is good for us as we experience the death of a loved one. Devine explains that Western culture applies a "forced happy outlook" on those who grieve, and it "glorifies transformation, while staunchly avoiding the reality of pain in the world" (p. 49). She offers a "new model of grief" in which she encourages the bereaved to let go of expectations placed on them for grieving: "I think all we can do, all any of us can do, is continue to be open about pain, death, grief, and love" (p. 79).

McInerny, N. (2019). *The hot young widows club: Lessons on survival from the front lines of grief.* New York: TED Books / Simon & Schuster.

Here's one of my favorite lines from this short little gem of a book by Nora McInerny: "I will confess right now that I do not love when people compare them losing their pet bird to me losing my husband, but then . . . I've never lost a bird" (p. 3). The book is less than a hundred pages long, with lots of sharp wit and humor. McInerny's purpose is to help anyone who grieves, but she speaks from the experience of being a widow.

CHAPTER 4

~~Happy~~ Holidays!

How to Cope with Celebrations

Tradition doesn't have to be perfect.

—Eleanor Haley, "New Perspective on
Old Traditions: Grief and the Holidays"
(2014)

Are there some days on the calendar that you would like to erase now that you are a WWPD? Which holidays or special occasions would you like to bypass? All of them?

What do you do when everyone is celebrating and you're alone?

There's nothing like holidays to make clear the reality of loss. Thankfully, sometimes the anticipation of coping with those holidays while grieving can be much worse than the actual events—much like the root canal or colonoscopy that keeps you up worrying at night but turns out to be not so bad after all. And it's helpful to remember that any holiday is just another day that only lasts twenty-four hours.

Of course, if it was truly just another day, it wouldn't be so hard to deal with.

Let's face it—holidays and special occasions will never be the same now that your partner is gone. My hope is that this chapter gives you some ideas for adding some humor to these days to make them a little better—or at least more tolerable.

MY STORY: DREADING THE "MOST WONDERFUL TIME OF THE YEAR"

My husband loved Christmas, and it was a big deal in our house. Tim was Santa for many people. He shopped for months to get just the right gifts for all the members of his large extended family. He spent days helping to decorate and wrap gifts.

I absolutely dreaded the first Christmas without him.

The sights, sounds, and smells of Christmas started rolling in around the middle of October, and I turned it off wherever I could. I didn't watch TV, I tried to ignore Christmas decorations displayed at the store, and I enlisted help with buying and wrapping gifts. However, my family and I decided to keep our traditions as close to "normal" as possible. Our decorations went up, we made plans to do our annual Christmas Eve trek to Tim's family's farm for dinner, and we ate the usual favorite cookies baked by my mother-in-law.

Christmas cards began arriving in the mail around the first week of December. Many cards contained thoughtful, heartfelt notes. (After a while, though, I felt as if I was getting sympathy cards all over again!) One evening, as I opened a pile of cards and bills, one envelope, containing what promised to be a Christmas card, caught my eye. I almost missed it. The envelope was addressed to Mr. and Mrs. Nettles.

But "Mr." was crossed out.

I was stunned and still shake my head in disbelief. (It's kind of funny now.)

I hope this type of thing never happens to you, but my guess is that you have some sort of similar story to tell. In this chapter, I'll share some ways to make any of your holidays a little more joyful—or at least tolerable—by intentionally looking for ways to smile and laugh during times that trigger sadness for so many WWPDs.

More than five years after Tim passed away, our family still struggles a bit with the Christmas season. Trying to keep the atmosphere festive and merry can be a chore, and sometimes the harder we try, the less cheery we become. Traditions that were once treasured now seem to be ugly reminders of what we've lost. Yet we were reluctant to change those traditions, because once we did, it felt like we were experiencing the death all over again.

In "After a Death, the Holidays Are a Secondary Loss," Eleanor Haley (2021) says that holidays become "secondary losses" after your loved one dies, because their absence changes or even erases the old way of observing and celebrating. Lucy Hone's advice in *Resilient Grieving* (2017) is to identify those secondary losses that mean the most to you. As a WWPD, you may have lots of them, in every facet of your life together. (One that stood out to me immediately, as I mentioned in Chapter 2, was the loss of my laundry person!) Hone suggests talking to someone about your secondary losses, or writing them down, which enables you to be more aware of them, figure out ways to cope with them, and get help from others as needed.

I found that the loss of our usual Christmas celebration was one of the hardest secondary losses for me—for everyone in our family—to cope with. It's difficult to inject humor into this type of loss.

I still contend that it feels better to laugh—or at least smile—than to cry.

HOW TO COPE WITH HOLIDAYS AND CELEBRATIONS

So, how can you make life better if you're dealing with the loss of your partner during a holiday? How can you manage sorrow while you're trying to make it through the merriment?

Try to look for opportunities to laugh or smile. In fact, you may need to make those opportunities happen. Here are some suggestions.

Declare Your Right to Switch Up Traditions

If your family has a tradition that you cherish, it's probably for good reason. You don't have to give it up entirely just because your partner died. See if you can modify it some way that feels good to you.

In my case, that first Christmas was a huge challenge for me. While I wanted to remember Tim at Christmastime, I didn't want a funeral atmosphere for the holiday. So I made memorial gifts for each family member, in memory of Tim, to open *before* Christmas day. These gifts were simple things like framed photos matted with fabric from his shirts, a watch of his that I had engraved for my sons, and little shadow boxes I made from some of his things I found in his desk drawers, such as a key chain, business cards, photos, golf tees, and concert tickets. They were separate from what was under the tree; I wanted to be able to honor Tim but also honor my own feelings about needing a little distance from the usual Christmas tradition. In this way, we were able to share a few memories and tears in a different space, while still allowing the usual Christmas celebration to continue relatively unchanged.

Is there some way you might imagine adding on to a beloved tradition? Or put your own spin on a celebration? Or start a new celebration entirely? You might find comfort in making just a small change or two in the way you've done things in the past.

Read Funny Books About Holidays

If you love to read, you can spend some time with some funny books that poke fun at holidays. Some suggestions are:

> *The Shepherd, the Angel, and Walter the Christmas*
> *Miracle Dog* by Dave Barry
> *Skipping Christmas* by John Grisham
> *A Christmas Blizzard* by Garrison Keillor
> *Wishin' and Hopin'* by Wally Lamb

Make Your Partner Part of the Festivities

Maybe honoring your partner is what you really want to do. (Not everyone feels this way, and that's okay!) If so, consider ways to have them be a presence. For example, every year since that first difficult Christmas, I have given gifts to members of my family that I know Tim would likely have picked out himself. He would have delighted in giving his granddaughter a toy drum (so it would create lots of noise for her parents to endure) and a case of dozens of Matchbox cars for his grandson (so they can be scattered all over the room, including in the cushions of the couch), so I bought these and gifted them. I actually prefer this method now, because I feel as if he is shopping with me, and if I'm not sure which thing to get, I just defer to whatever I think he'd choose.

There are other ways you might honor your partner: Tell the jokes they would typically share; make a toast using words they would likely impart for the occasion; bring a framed picture of them to the event (you could even set a notebook beside it and ask people to share thoughts, especially if the crowd is close family); play a game they would have liked to play, whether poker or musical chairs or badminton; make their favorite dish. There are many ways to honor a person. And don't hesitate to ask for ideas from loved ones if you're in brain-fog mode.

Give Yourself a Movie Night

Pop some popcorn, settle in on the couch, and watch a humorous movie about any holiday that you dread. (All of them, if necessary!) Here are a few suggestions.

Christmas

> *A Christmas Story* (1983)
> *Christmas in Connecticut* (1945)
> *Christmas with the Kranks* (2004)
> *Deck the Halls* (2006)
> *Elf* (2003)
> *Grumpy Old Men* (1993)
> *Home Alone* (1990)
> *National Lampoon's Christmas Vacation* (1989)
> *Scrooged* (1988)
> *The Santa Clause* (1994)
> *Trading Places* (1983)

Hanukkah

> *Little Fockers* (2010)
> *Eight Crazy Nights* (2002)

Thanksgiving

Funny Thing About Love (2021)
The Turkey Bowl (2019)
Friendsgiving (2020)

Father's Day

Grown Ups (2010)
Father's Day (1997)
Raising Arizona (1987)

Easter

Easter Sunday (2022)

Fourth of July

American Graffiti (1973)
1776 (1972)
The Sandlot (1993)

Valentine's Day

How to Lose a Guy in 10 Days (2003)
10 Things I Hate About You (1999)
Girlfriend's Day (2017)
Love, Guaranteed (2020)

Make Other Plans

You do not have to spend any holiday alone, if you don't want
to. Nor do you have to spend it with others, if you don't want

to. Do what you want to do. Focus on making yourself feel better and on making your life a little bit easier. Here are some holiday-specific suggestions.

Birthdays

Birthdays are tough. It was a few days before Tim's birthday, the first year he was gone, and I ordered butterflies. My granddaughter and my mother-in-law helped me release them in my backyard. I had to focus on the logistics of opening the box, pulling out the little pods that contained butterflies, and explain to a three-year-old and an eighty-five-year-old what we were doing. Eventually, all the butterflies fluttered about, but the best part was laughing about how we couldn't convince, at first, the darn things to take flight.

The next day, I went to Florida to be with my mother, whose birthday is the same as Tim's. At first, I felt guilty about leaving my family on that day. But I decided that I needed to concentrate on celebrating someone who is still here—my eighty-year-old mother. Since that time, I've found places other than home to be on Tim's birthday. I always put out a social media post that marks the day, with a photo and a few words about Tim, then I do something I enjoy.

Maybe you can find something fun to do that day. Acknowledge the day, but do something that makes you smile.

Christmas

If Christmas carols don't cheer you up, just don't listen to them. Listen to upbeat songs that make you want to dance.

Ask someone to help you wrap gifts. On that first Christmas without Tim, one of his cousins, who is also a good friend, drove across town to help me wrap gifts that Tim had already bought for family members. We poured a glass of wine, said a toast to Tim, and wrapped everything up while we shared stories about some of our crazy family members.

Focus on others. Get involved with the great variety of opportunities to make the holidays happier for other people. Homeless centers and nursing homes are filled with people who could use some positivity. Help some families who are less fortunate, if you can. When you're hurting, it's easy to forget about how good it feels to think about somebody else during this time.

Easter

This Christian holiday also signals the start of spring. Even the fresh new beginnings of leaves reappearing and flowers budding can be depressingly cruel to the WWPD, who wants nothing more than a rebirth she cannot have.

The year after my husband died, my family attended an Easter brunch at a local restaurant. I hadn't wanted to go, because events like this often reminded me of Tim's absence. But I felt it was important to my family for me to be there, so I went. During the meal, a large Easter Bunny worked the crowd, stopping at each table, visiting with the children and giving their parents photo opportunities. This tall, furry, masked character was a little bit imposing to Charlotte, my three-year-old granddaughter, but she tolerated him well and obliged when her mother took a photo of her with the Easter Bunny. However, as soon as the photo was taken, she gestured to the character with a dismissing wave and said, "You can hop along now!"

The image of a large, imposing Easter Bunny who was told to "hop along" by a three-year-old has become an inside family joke. I've shared the story with dozens of friends, too. From that time on, whenever I encounter an ugly, imposing thought about the sadness that a holiday brings me (or actually any ugly thought that I just don't want to deal with at the moment), I try to remember that little three-year-old face with a strong, firm voice that said, "You can hop along now!"

Maybe it will work for you, too. Try visualizing the things that trouble you. Put them in a large and ridiculous costume, and get rid of them for now. Simply reducing the menacing thoughts to something manageable that you can dismiss, even just momentarily, might help when you're facing a struggle over a holiday.

Thanksgiving

Does the empty chair at the table for Thanksgiving dinner make you want to cry instead of eat? Then don't do it. A friend of mine has lost every member of her immediate family—her parents, her brother, her sister. She's the only one left. She now makes a meal on the Sunday before Thanksgiving and invites friends to join her. Thus, Thanksgiving Day, she says, is just another day.

Would you rather enjoy sushi and sake with some friends? Then invite them over on Saturday, when everyone is sick of turkey anyway, and order in the chef's special sushi rolls.

Valentine's Day

This day might be the cruelest day of the year for the WWPD. Not getting flowers, cards, candy, or going out to fancy dinners can be stark reminders of what you've lost.

I suggest that you buy yourself some flowers, if you like them (and you're not allergic!). You can pick them up at the grocery store. Don't worry about getting a big fancy bouquet of roses. Just get something cheerful. Display them prominently.

Or, if flowers aren't your thing, treat yourself to a piece of decadent candy (oh, okay, go ahead and have the whole box) or a nice dinner, even if it's takeout. You can ask a close friend or family member to have dinner with you.

Perhaps you can send some Valentine cards to senior citizens at a local memory-care center.

Do you have a special Valentine's Day memory? There's no reason you can't cherish it and enjoy thinking about the love you and your partner shared. One of my favorite memories is this one: Tim was not one for romantic love letters or cards, although he did send flowers frequently, for no reason at all. But on the Valentine's Day before he died (which happened to be a day and a half before he died), he gave me a card. It was a cute, funny one, and he wrote, *Here's your card. Sorry I forgot to give it to you last year.* He had bought the card, put it in the glove box of his car for safekeeping, and then forgot about it for a year. Of course, now it's one of my most treasured keepsakes.

One trick for helping to ease the pain of Valentine's Day is to do a little mind exercise. Look around you for examples of love. What kinds of love can you find? A sunset, a toddler playing with his mother, a child laughing at a "knock-knock" joke, a fluttering butterfly, your dog resting at your bedside, a smile from a stranger, and a grocery clerk saying, "Have a nice day" can all be examples of love, when you think about it. You don't need flowers and candy to realize those things.

Anniversaries

How long were you with your partner? What's your anniversary date? Now that your partner is gone, it probably feels impossible to celebrate. Going to dinner (or quite frankly, doing *anything*) alone punctuates the awful feeling that your partner isn't there to celebrate with you. Yet ignoring the day altogether is also impossible.

It is probably not a good day to be alone. Try to plan ahead so that you aren't stuck with nothing to do. Seek the company of others. Go somewhere. Can you get out of town? Or stay local and go someplace where you can enjoy being with friends or family. Do something very un-anniversary-like—perhaps something you and your partner never did together. Camping? Antiquing? Boating? The rodeo? Shopping? The art museum? Pickleball? It might help to use this day as an opportunity to do something very new and renew a vow—with your new, strong, bad-ass self.

And here's a new anniversary—the day your partner died. Is that date forever stuck in the calendar of your mind? Now you have a new anniversary to worry about. Here's a day where you can do the opposite. Engage in something that you and your partner enjoyed. Did you travel together? Then plan a trip—either far away or locally. Did you play sports together? Then go to a game or match. Or spend it with family members and do things such as eat your partner's favorite meal, make a toast with your partner's favorite drink, or wear your partner's favorite color. Whatever you do, recognize that this day is now an important part of your life.

MY SECRET SANTA

A few days before that first Christmas without Tim, I chatted with my friend Ginny about the tradition of Christmas stockings in our house. I told her about how, every year, I was the one in charge of making sure stockings for everyone in the family had at least a few things stuffed in them. Tim took care of the big things around the tree, so I always put a couple of little things in everyone's stocking—little toys, candy, cologne, and the like. But somehow, even though Tim never admitted to doing it, I always found something small in my stocking. I told her that I would sorely miss seeing the little lump in my stocking this year.

Yet, when I woke up Christmas morning in 2018, I discovered that my stocking was full. I later found out that Ginny (who had a key to my house) had snuck into the house before sunrise and filled my stocking with a variety of nice, cheerful things. I am still amazed at how she got into the house and filled my stocking without anyone knowing.

For the first time since I was a child, I actually wondered if Santa had, indeed, squeezed his way down my chimney. It certainly made me smile.

Do whatever you can to keep yourself in a positive state of mind on any holiday or celebration. Truth is you won't be able wipe those holidays off the calendar, no matter how much you want to. And you might not be the lucky recipient of a secret Santa. But you can look for reasons to smile and provide smiles for others. As Erma Bombeck said, "If you can't make it better, you can laugh at it" (Lazear & Lazear, 1993).

And, if all else fails, you can remind yourself that it's just another day.

RESOURCES THAT HELPED ME MANAGE HOLIDAYS AND CELEBRATIONS

https://whatsyourgrief.com

What's Your Grief is a website devoted to providing resources to "finding ways to function in a world turned on its head." Under the tab Grief Articles, there's an entire section called "Holidays and Special Days," which leads you to a list of excellent blogs that focus on dealing with celebrations. This website does give readers the opportunity to leave comments. As with any forum in which people may post online, either anonymously or not, remember that grief is quite personal. I've found that some sites can actually be depressing because comments are either overwhelmingly sad or sometimes downright cruel. I haven't experienced such difficult reading on the What's Your Grief site. In fact, the authors of the site are compassionate and empathetic in their replies to comments, while offering lots of resourceful information to their readers.

CHAPTER 5

I Don't Wanna!

How to Get Your Affairs in Order

In three words, I can sum up everything I've learned about life: It goes on.

—Robert Frost, quoted in the *Cincinnati Enquirer* (Josephs, 1954)

It's bad enough to lose your life partner. But you may have discovered that you also have to, while coping with deep grief, take care of all kinds of things you never dreamed you would need to do, such as pay funeral bills, sort through medical bills, find passwords, close bank accounts, order a grave monument, talk to lawyers, and file life insurance claims. The list goes on and on.

On top of all that, you may be working outside the home, taking care of your children (even the adult children need your attention—they're grieving, too), or caring for your aging parents.

And maybe you have found that there are so many other

important things to do, which you have absolutely no motivation to do. What did your partner do for you and your household? Mow the grass? Change the oil in the car? Do the grocery shopping? Walk the dog? Fix the leaky toilet? File your taxes?

The tricky thing about becoming a WWPD is that death has taken your partner, and now you're grieving the loss of the role your partner played in your life, and that can make you grieve for a way of life that is now gone and become absolutely overwhelmed at all the things you must now do alone. (We touched on this in Chapter 1.)

Sound familiar?

Oh, and to add to that—you've got "widow's brain," where all of a sudden, you have trouble remembering simple things, you feel as if you're in a fog all the time, and you're completely exhausted most of the day. (It's only supposed to last about a year, but it's been five years for me and I still forget things and want to take a nap on occasion. So I'm milking this "widow's brain" thing as long as I can.)

In this chapter, you'll learn some ideas for making your life a tiny bit simpler, and maybe even more tolerable, during these awful days.

MY STORY: JUST ONE PHONE CALL

We were having dinner at our favorite local restaurant, sharing our day's events with each other. Tim had had a follow-up meeting with our financial advisor that afternoon. He told me—and these were his exact words—"Well, it's all set. If I get hit by that proverbial bus tomorrow, all you have to do is make one phone call. Everything is taken care of for you."

And to think all I had to share was how well my class went that day.

He didn't get hit by a bus the next day, but he did have a

sudden massive heart attack about three years later. And while it was quite a bit more complicated than making one phone call, I was extremely lucky in that I had someone guide me through the process of collecting life insurance benefits, settling the estate, making a plan for my financial future, and reorganizing my own end-of-life wishes. My financial advisor was a lifesaver during those very difficult days when even the tiniest and most familiar details were murky in my foggy brain.

But everyone's situation is different, making the process of getting financial and other practical matters in order a unique and complex experience.

HOW TO HANDLE WHAT YOU'D RATHER PUT OFF FOREVER

Your situation may be more complex than the scope of this book allows. There are other books that do an outstanding job of helping you through that process. I highly recommend that you seek out these resources if you're in the position of settling your partner's estate on your own; these books are listed at the end of the chapter.

Here are a few practical tips that might help you keep your sanity during this nightmarish process of managing life without your partner.

Review What You've Got

It is crucial to make an inventory of all your financial assets and liabilities, including any life insurance benefits for which you are eligible. This inventory is your balance sheet. Find a professional that you trust to work with—an attorney, financial advisor, or CPA (certified public accountant). With them, make this list, and then ask questions! Are there any items you do not understand? Any vocabulary, acronyms, or terms you've never heard of or have forgotten altogether? Find out what everything means, and ask these people to write it down for you. And if you forget, lose your notes, or still don't understand, ask again!

You may also need help in finding assets, especially if your partner took care of such details. Life insurance policies have a way of hiding if you don't know about them. Check the Human Resources Office at their place of work and yours, too. You might have a policy that you or your partner has been paying for through automatic deductions from your paycheck.

Understand Your New Cash Flow

All your future sources of income and expenses are part of your cash flow. Cash flow is certainly affected by the death of your partner. Social Security, pensions, and living expenses are a few of the items that should be reviewed and analyzed. If you don't already have one, find a financial advisor who can provide comprehensive financial planning services, which will be a great asset when examining your cash flow and creating a budget for your new life going forward.

You may feel a need to regain some control over your life. This feeling might translate to paying off all credit card debts or car loans, or relocating, or paying off your mortgage. Talk to an advisor who can help you make a plan.

Give yourself some grace. When I first became a WWPD, I was scared to death of making a mistake financially. Tim and I paid bills and balanced the checkbook together, so I was familiar with his method of doing things. He used to balance the checkbook to the penny, using an old adding machine. He also saved every tiny piece of paper and receipt, filing them in a large box alphabetically. I tried to duplicate his methods, because, after all, they worked pretty well for him. But the old adding machine and I didn't get along well, and besides, with electronic banking, everything was added and subtracted for me. And I began to run out of room for all the boxes of files filled with old receipts. So I learned to trust myself and adapt to my own style of doing things. You can do this, too. Whatever your partner handled, there is an internet search term for it, and you can educate yourself. And don't be shy about asking for help.

Order Extra Copies of Your . . .

Marriage certificate? No. Well, that's important, too, but I'm referring to that nasty little thing called a death certificate. Trust me, you will need more than you thought you would need. The life insurance company, credit card companies, banks, and title companies (the list goes on and on) all need to see this document to verify that your partner has died. The problem is these pieces of paper are expensive—in some cases, around ten dollars per copy. Do it. Buy more than you want to buy—at least twenty-five of them—and keep them on file.

Here's a story about that death certificate: About three weeks after Tim died, he received a jury duty summons in the mail. At first, I was tempted to toss it in the trash. But I didn't want to keep getting mail addressed to him. So I opened the form only to realize that there was no box to check off that said, "Deceased." So I wrote a brief note to explain the situation and sent it to the clerk of the county courthouse, along with a copy of Tim's death certificate.

About two weeks later, I received a lovely note from the clerk, offering her sympathies. She also sent the death certificate back, saying, *I know these things are expensive. Please keep it.*

That is one very thoughtful person.

And speaking of the marriage certificate, look yours up and have copies of it available, too. You will need it.

Learn from Trusted Sources and Write Everything Down

Talk to people you trust. Likewise, use your instincts. If you don't trust them, then don't rely on them. And when you do talk to your life insurance agent, or your lawyer, or your any-one at the bank regarding your financial situation or your partner's estate, write it down. Keep a notebook or set of files, alphabetized by category. Ask for and write down the name of anyone you talk to who gives you information, advice, or direction.

Go to Retail Therapy—Carefully

I am now the proud owner of several lovely dresses that I prob-ably will never wear. Why? Because, in the beginning of my life as a WWPD, buying something new felt so good, whether I needed it or not.

Yes, retail therapy is a "thing" for many WWPDs. Some WWPDs also spend time and money remodeling their living spaces—or at least changing some aspect of a room or two—with new pillows, a fresh coat of paint, or a couple of new pic-tures on the wall.

Perhaps it's because buying tangible items or changing the decor helps us feel more in control. Perhaps it simply feels good to pamper ourselves. Regardless, be careful! It's easy to spend too much money at this time of your vulnerability. One way to curb your appetite is to work toward paying off all your credit card accounts and then closing them—except one. Keep one credit card account for purchasing everything, but pay off the balance each month. Getting rid of your debt is smart, especially now. But just as importantly, forcing yourself to pay off your balance will help keep your spending in control.

Keep a List (or Maybe Lots of Lists)

If you are like I was and can't trust your memory about anything, it's time to write things down. I know this sounds so obvious, but if you are used to being the one that everyone relies on to remember everything from birthdays to dentist appointments, you may be utterly frustrated that you can't even remember to bring in the mail. Please be kind to yourself. You have just gone through a traumatic event and your brain isn't functioning the way it used to.

What worked for me was writing a single task on a sticky note. Some of these notes were ridiculously simple, such as "Pack tomorrow's lunch" or "Put gas in the car." I stuck them to a pretty tray, which became my "Sticky Note Central." I carried the tray from room to room, adding notes as I thought of something I needed to do. And if anyone asked me if there was anything they could do, I took a look at the sticky notes on the tray and gave them a task. (I quickly found out who really meant it when they said, "Let me know if there's something I can do!")

So as elementary as this piece of advice sounds, keep a list—in whatever fashion suits you. There are just too many things going on in this new phase of your life (including the fact that your brain doesn't quite function as it used to), so do yourself a favor and write down your to-dos. Keep your list—or your dozens of sticky notes—in the same place so you always know where it is. Your phone can be an excellent receptacle for such notes.

Enlist the Help of an Organizer—or Two

Find someone to help you get organized. You might need help with things that ordinarily would not bother you at all, such as cleaning out a closet, taking things to a donation center, decorating for a holiday, or grocery shopping.

I hired the daughter of a friend to do things for me. She made phone calls, organized the garage (which was now minus one car with lots of space for junk to accumulate), cleaned out Tim's office, put old photos in albums, and did some shopping for me. She was a lifesaver.

If you can't or don't want to hire someone, perhaps a close friend or family member can help you. A wonderful friend of mine, Jodi, visited for a week and helped me figure out what to do with social media accounts and lost passwords. She also helped me clean out one of Tim's closets, where we found some bags of T-shirts and socks he had bought on sale— unworn, with price tags and receipts attached. Even though they had been in the closet for a while, she took these back to the store, explained that the buyer had passed away, and got my money back. That task was something I never would've been able to do myself.

No matter how long it's been since your partner died, there's always something that needs to be organized, cleaned out, or managed. Look around. What's been bugging you? What have you been procrastinating? What task do you need help with? If you don't have family or friends that can help, who can you hire? Social media offers many opportunities to find volunteers or paid helpers. Teens or college students can be excellent choices for help in managing lots of things you don't want to do.

Got a Honey-Do List? Google It

Did your partner take care of some tasks that leave you clueless? Was your household managed through honey-do lists? Most couples get everyday life done through individual efforts that contribute to meeting the overall team goal; for example, one person does yardwork while the other does housework.

Now that you're doing the work of both members of the team, it's common for very simple things to become overwhelming. (I know a WWPD who had never filled her own car with gas.)

Thank goodness for Google and YouTube! These resources can help you figure out just about anything: hanging pictures, fixing a leaky faucet, draining the pool, cooking dinner, starting the lawn mower, doing the laundry . . . The list goes on and on.

Yet there are some things I've not yet figured out how to do. I've never bought my own car. I still haven't used a snowblower. And I absolutely cannot figure out how to work the TV remote.

So give yourself a break. Some things will simply need to wait. You don't have to do everything right away. Tackle one small task at a time, and bask in the glow of self-pride when you do finally figure it out.

Pass It On: Make Your Last Wishes Known Now

Experiencing the death of my husband changed my perspective on life. I learned that, in spite of the fact that Tim had done a very good job of preparing me for life without him, I still wasn't fully prepared for the life-altering and mind-boggling loss. Additionally, I had to force myself to come to grips with my own mortality and think about how I could make things a little easier for my family once my time comes.

I encourage you, if you haven't already, to give your afterlife some thought. What do you want your loved ones to do? What have you learned from your experience? Tell them. Here are some suggestions:

- Make sure you have an advance directive, or living will, to make clear to your loved ones what kind of end-of-life medical care you want.
- Choose a durable power of attorney, or a healthcare surrogate, so that you will have someone to speak for you if you cannot.
- Update your estate plan. You'll need to retitle any financial accounts that were held jointly. You might need to amend beneficiaries. Review your will and determine a power of attorney. An estate attorney will be able to guide you through this process.
- If it matters to you, be explicit about what you would like at your funeral or celebration of life. Be reasonable, too. Remember that grieving makes everything twice as hard to do and some requests just simply cannot be done. Give your loved ones permission to memorialize you in positive ways that will make them feel better.
- Write a letter of last instruction, which is an informal letter that supplements your will. (You can Google this letter and obtain a form letter to adapt.) Contents of this letter should make things easier for your loved ones as they take care of your estate. You'll need to list things such as personal contacts, usernames and passwords for your online accounts, locations of important documents, a list of any personal artifacts that you wish to bestow to others (which may not be listed in your

will), instructions for pets, and what to do with
your social media accounts or pages. Be sure to
sign it and have it notarized. Then give it to your
trusted loved ones.

- Don't be afraid to include some humor in your
letter. Adding a favorite family "inside joke,"
funny photos you want to be sure to pass on, or
one of those "in ten years this will be funny" stories will help your family. (Review and update this
letter yearly.)

SPEAKING OF THOSE LAST WISHES . . .

Even though my husband died suddenly, I knew his afterlife
wishes very well. We had discussed this subject several times.
Because he wanted to be cremated, and he had given me a list
of places to bury his ashes, I bought several small urns from
the funeral home, each filled with his ashes. (As I told many of
my friends and family who asked about this situation, "There
was plenty of Tim to go around.")

But I found out the hard way (literally) that spreading
cremated ashes is not as easy as it sounds. That first summer
after he died, I gathered a circle of friends on the dock at a
close friend's lake house. This lake was Tim's favorite place to
go for vacation; these people were some of his favorite people.
We were going to sprinkle his ashes in the lake. Only problem was his ashes had become hardened, like plaster of paris,
in this urn. Finally, my friend Colleen took off her sunglasses
and used the frame to chisel some ashes out of the urn, saying,
"Dammit, Tim, stop being so stubborn!" We all shared a good
laugh. It certainly broke up a very tense moment.

So here's one last reminder: If you want to be cremated

with your ashes spread somewhere, remind your loved ones to make sure you're loose and spreadable before the ceremony.

RESOURCES THAT HELPED ME WITH PRACTICAL STUFF I DIDN'T WANT TO DO

Armstrong, A., & Donahue, M. (2012). *On your own: A widow's passage to emotional and financial well-being* (5th ed.). Washington, DC: On Your Own Publishing Company, LLC.

The authors present advice on all facets of managing finances, using a unique point of view—your personality traits. The way money has influenced your life from childhood will affect the way you respond to the situation in which you now find yourself. They also present four hypothetical widows, whose stories are based on the experiences of real people, and throughout the book they explain how these widows reacted to the process of getting their lives back together again. Someone who is also a WWPD gave me this book shortly after my husband died. I'll admit—at 403 pages, this book was a bit overwhelming at first. But its straightforward explanations of terms and concepts have really helped me, even five years after my husband's death.

Meekhoff, K., & Windell, J. (2015). *A widow's guide to healing: Gentle support and advice for the first five years.* Naperville, IL: Sourcebooks.

This book is chock-full of suggestions for helping the WWPD get back on her feet; it's an excellent, practical source that might serve as a handbook to a widow. Chapter 6, "Facing Finances Without Fear," gives advice on things such as finding where your financial assets are— there are so many surprises for the WWPD! Chapter 9 offers a checklist to help you get started with a "game plan" for your future.

Oh No, I'm Having a Moment!

How to Handle Grief Triggers

> What really matters, in terms of our long-term health, is the ability to crack a grin when the chips are down.
>
> —George Bonanno, *The Other Side of Sadness: What the New Science of Bereavement Tells Us About Life After Loss*
> (2019)

People say that grief hits at odd moments; the tiniest little reminders of the departed loved one will leave you in an emotional crumple on the floor. (It can certainly lead to some embarrassing, ugly-cry moments!)

Have you experienced these "triggers," where the grief is so debilitating that it stops everything and time freezes? Awful, isn't it, to be living life normally, with everything going along just fine, and then suddenly, one of your senses becomes aware of something that reminds you of your loss? Then, boom, there goes that nice day you were having.

Try as we might to build a habit of a little cheer for each day (which is what Chapter 2 is all about), these waves of grief can wash over us without warning. What are your triggers? And how can humor and positivity help you cope with those moments? In this chapter, you'll learn tried-and-true strategies for riding out the grief wave.

MY STORY: TRIGGERED BY THE LAST BIT OF TIDE

My husband was a coupon clipper and shopped at the drugstore for BOGO bargains. He stockpiled essentials such as toilet paper, shampoo, and of course, laundry detergent. We had dozens of bottles of detergent in our laundry room. About two years after he passed away, I finally came upon the last bottle of Tide. When I poured that last cupful into the washing machine, I sobbed.

I'd been told the second year after his death would be worse than the first. On that day, I realized that this was true. Tim was truly gone forever. I missed him terribly anyway, but adding to that pain was the reminder that, once again, I was on my own. This was painful, but it also made me angry. I shouted, "Dammit, Tim! Now what am I going to do?"

It took a few days, but finally I went to the store for more detergent. I told all of this to the clerk when I checked out about ten bottles of Tide—all purchased on sale.

"When I talk to him again, I'm going to give him an earful. He knows I don't like shopping for this stuff," I said to her.

She looked at me sideways, uncomfortably realized I was joking, and cautiously smiled. It did make me feel better, though. I felt a tiny wave of relief at my own joke, picked up my treasure trove of Tide bottles, and left the store feeling a little bit stronger.

As time moves on and my husband's death becomes part

of my history, I contend that it's a shame to have bad days. Do I have bad moments? Yes—I allow myself whatever bad moments I need to feel the pain of grief, because grief must be recognized. It still happens on a regular basis, even after all these years. I've found that the saddest part of my loss now is how Tim's absence affects my children and grandchildren. The loss of their father and grandfather has left enormous gaps in their lives, and as years pass, the loss seems even greater than it was before. Every time I think about this loss—and the thought pops into my brain frequently—deep pain stops me in my tracks, no matter where I am or what I'm doing.

I can tolerate a moment or two of grief, even on a daily basis. But I cannot allow my grief to consume whole days. Life is too short to let a whole day go by without enjoying a laugh.

HOW TO GET THROUGH TRIGGERS AND DARK DAYS

How can you add positivity and humor to your life when the grief surges at random? Shown below are some ideas that I have tried and liked.

Put a Pen in Your Mouth (I'm Serious—Try It!)

So, you *really* don't feel like smiling? Here's a very easy trick: Fool your brain into thinking that you *do* feel like smiling. How? By putting a pen in your mouth! Why? In research done on the effects of doing things that the brain associates with happiness (Strack et al., 1988), researchers asked participants of two groups to each hold a pen in their mouth. One group was to hold the pen as if sucking on a straw or smoking a cigarette, which forces the lips to frown. The other group was asked to hold the pen horizontally in the mouth, which creates the shape of a smile. Participants in the "smiling" group were the ones who found cartoons to be funnier and seemed to feel happier as a result. The study reinforced the idea that the human brain responds to physical stimulus from the body.

Thus, according to this research, if you physically make yourself smile by biting down on a pen, you'll feel a little bit better, if only for a moment. I'm not saying that you should go around faking a smile all the time and ignoring what you really feel. But sometimes, when you simply feel awful, you need a little bit of relief, even if it's only for a moment.

I tried this little trick, and it worked for me. It may seem silly to you, and I don't think it will work in every situation, but it's worth a try.

Play Some Cheerful Tunes

Listen to music that makes you smile, snap your fingers, and want to dance. Collect these songs and play at least one of them daily. Songs like these can bring a smile to your face for just a few minutes, even when you don't feel like smiling: "Don't Worry Be Happy" by Bobby McFerrin, "What a Wonderful World" by Louis Armstrong, "Lovely Day" by Bill Withers, "Happy" by Pharrell Williams, or one of my favorites, "Kokomo" by the Beach Boys. There are lots of lists of positive songs online—just do a simple online search and you'll find songs you may have forgotten or didn't even know about.

Tell People What You Need (Even If It Makes No Sense)

Don't wait for people to guess. Tell them what you need. Don't worry about how much sense it makes to others. If you can't think of anything because it's just too hard to think, that's okay, too. But if something is important to you, then speak up.

Here's an example: Our family had a holiday tradition that was Tim's favorite thing to do—we hung wreaths on every window in the house. (I'm quite certain Tim was the only one in the family who actually enjoyed this project.) It took hours to put them up—and weeks to take them down. We usually just left them up during the Pittsburgh winter months and then got them down sometime in March. Thus, when Tim died in mid-February, those wreaths were still on display. The day after he died, inexplicably, I decided that the wreaths must come down. I said to my twenty-three-year-old son, Tommy, "I need for you to take down those wreaths." He did, indeed, look at me like I was crazy. But he enlisted help from some friends, and they took them down.

Another example happened during our annual trip to Disney World. Our first trip without Tim also happened to be the first time I sat in the back seat, between my grandchildren, tears streaming down my face. It was no one's fault, but I just got the awful feeling that I didn't belong there. In my mind, I belonged in the front seat, with Tim driving and our grown children and their children in the back seat.

I said, "I need to rent my own car." And from that time on, I rented my own car to accompany the family on vacation. Besides that, it helped to have extra trunk room for all the luggage required for a family with toddlers.

To facilitate getting the help she needed, one WWPD created a "repair fund" from her late husband's life insurance money. Whenever she asked for help with repairs in the house but didn't get it from her grown children, she hired someone to do it for her and paid the hired help from this fund. She told her children that their inheritance was being spent on hired help. Indeed, she started getting more help with repairs around the house.

It doesn't matter if you make sense or not. If you're not getting the help you want, ask for it. Tell the people who are close to you what you need.

Cue Up the Comedy

Look up stand-up acts. My favorites run the gamut and include Carol Burnett, Betty White, Dave Barry, Alan Alda, Robin Williams, Will Rogers, Dorothy Parker, Jim Gaffigan, Amy Schumer, Kevin Hart, Ali Wong, Trey Kennedy, and Nate Bargatze. It's easy to find them on YouTube or streaming networks. Compiling these in one place, such as your favorites list, helps because if you wait until you're feeling depressed to find something to watch, you probably won't.

Revisit Those Childhood Comforts

What was your childhood like? If you have happy memories of a song, a comforting dish, a game you liked to play, or a book, bring these things back into your life. If only momentarily, you can feel comfort from them and maybe even smile as you remember them.

For example, one of my fondest memories of childhood is playing tennis in the street in front of our house. There was very little traffic on this suburban drive, and my sisters and I chalked lines on the street for an imaginary net. We played with the neighborhood kids every late summer afternoon, stopping only for dinner and the inevitable streetlight that turned on, which meant we had to go inside. Fast-forward about fifty years or so: In the past couple of years, I've thoroughly enjoyed taking tennis lessons. I believe I play about as well as I did then, but that doesn't matter. I like the challenge and the fact that hitting the ball successfully (on occasion) makes me smile.

Another WWPD sought light as her comfort. She said that suddenly she felt the need to sleep with a night-light on, just as she did when she was a child. Now that she is a WWPD, she keeps a small light on in nearly every room in her house. It doesn't make sense, but it doesn't have to.

Think back to your childhood. If there was something that brought you joy or comfort, bring it back. It might also bring back a smile or two.

Say Thank You, Thank You, Thank You

One of the things that might help you get through grief is gratitude. I know it sounds like a cliché; memes on social media everywhere implore us to have "an attitude of gratitude." Sometimes it's just hard to be grateful about anything when you feel like life has slapped you in the face—as, indeed, it did when your partner died and took away your plans for a life together.

During the first year of my grief, I wondered if maybe it couldn't hurt to give this gratitude thing a try. So I began to search my memory for people who have helped me in some way or another over the years, as far back as my childhood. I kept a list of these people, many of whom were long forgotten. Every day I made it a practice to write a short thank-you note to someone on that list. Some of these people were truly influential in my life, such as my high school English teacher, Miss Rodriguez; others were people I met in passing, such as the very kind woman who worked at the deli counter in my parents' neighborhood. I was surprised at how good it felt to let other people know how much they meant to me. I even received some notes in return, thanking me for the thank-you note! These notes helped me feel as if my life was not so bad after all. The act of practicing gratitude and the thought of putting a smile on someone else's face pulled me out of many sad moments.

You don't have to go on a letter-writing campaign. You can

text, call, or email people who have done something for you or influenced your life positively. You might find that the act of writing and sending a thank-you note can give you a brief break from feeling pain. You might get a little lift whenever you send a note to someone you haven't seen in a while just to say, "Hey—you're great. Thanks for being that."

Find the Good Stuff

Think about "benefit finding." This technique was described by psychologist Lucy Hone in *Resilient Grieving* (p. 179). It means to find something—anything—that is positive in your situation. Thinking about your loss in a flexible manner can help you cope. It doesn't mean that you are glad bad things have happened to you. Benefit finding means that you are accepting the reality and are looking at how your life can be okay even though it includes deep sadness.

And benefit finding doesn't have to be anything earth-shattering. I still whisper a little "thank you" to Tim every time I balance the checkbook, because he had organized our finances so thoroughly and insisted that we pay bills together each month so that I would have a finger on the pulse of our bank account. In a sense, he was preparing me for a life without him, and for that, I am grateful.

If you were to start making a list, what would be one tiny little good thing in your life? Can you list two or three?

Switch to Positive Self-Talk

At moments when you feel particularly vulnerable to grief, repeat this phrase to yourself: "I am _____." Fill in the blank with positive words only. For example, "I am intelligent. I am content. I am funny. I am settled. I am strong. I am okay." Just keep going with the positive self-talk as long as you can stand it. As you pat yourself on the back, you may find that you feel a tiny bit stronger as you power through tough moments.

LAUGHING WITHOUT GUILT

Above all, don't feel guilty about laughing. Laughing doesn't mean that you are "over" your loss or that you are disrespecting your dead partner. It means that you are living a life that includes joy, fun, and positivity, in spite of your loss. Laughing helps you power through all those bad moments, so go ahead and allow yourself to feel the relief.

When I'm feeling overwhelmed by the sadness of grieving, I try to remember Betty White, who lost the love of her life, Allen Ludden, after eighteen years of marriage. Yet she determined that it doesn't help to become a "professional mourner" (Bennett, 2011). Just as I give myself permission to cry, I also give myself permission to smile. I hope you can, too.

RESOURCES THAT HELPED ME WITH NAVIGATING TRIGGERS AND TOUGH MOMENTS

Stifter, K. (2020). *The funny thing about grief.* Saint Paul, MN: Beaver's Pond Press.

> *After Katie Stifter lost her husband in a drowning accident, she struggled to keep life as normal as possible for her children. She tells about how a positive outlook and a sense of humor helped get her through her darkest days. The title of Chapter 8, "Funeral Planning: My New Side Gig," gives an indication of her humorous style, alongside very practical chapters such as Chapter 11, "How to Help Someone Who Is Grieving." Stifter also gives testament to the power of her faith in*

coping with grief. Stifter is a younger widow with three young children, so she writes from that perspective.

Thompson, B. L. (2020). *Sudden widow: The story of love, grief, and recovery, and how badly it can suck!* New York: Brooklyn Writers Press.

In this short book (115 pages), author Bella Lynn Thompson gives an honest account of the events surrounding her husband's sudden and fatal heart attack at age forty-seven. While the focus is not on the use of humor to cope with the tragedy, Thompson does use wry humor to describe her new life, invoking instant empathy. For example, in Chapter 4, "Wanting to Smash Things," she writes, "I frequently say that when I get to heaven or wherever he is, I'll punch him first and hug him right after" (p. 35).

CHAPTER 7

A Widow Walks into a Bar

How to Step Out into the World Socially

Learning to laugh after a loss means being compassionate with yourself and the world around you.

—Allen Klein, *The Courage to Laugh: Humor, Hope, and Healing in the Face of Death and Dying* (1998)

As a member of a pair, you've lost your other half. If your social life included your partner (as it does with most married or committed couples), then you may have found that socializing came to a sudden halt when your partner died. It might even feel as if people just don't want to be around you anymore. Or it may feel like people have forgotten you. (Which could be true, because let's face it—the world grinds on and people, even the ones closest to you, are busy.)

Have you been able to go out to dinner alone? What about other things that you and your partner did together—are you able to still do those things? Do you still see the friends you used to hang out with when your partner was alive? Did some of them stop calling after the funeral or memorial was over?

It's a lonely feeling to realize that the world goes on without your partner—and without you. People you once socialized with suddenly disappear. They give parties and don't invite you. Weekends, which may have once been a time for fun-filled events, are now blank days and nights with nothing on the calendar.

The focus of this chapter is how to find your social self again: making friends, making connections, getting out of your living space, and cultivating more relationships that will carry you through the rest of your life. A large part of finding the new social you is becoming more comfortable with being by yourself. Thus, this chapter also explores how to enjoy solitude and grow from it—or how to be alone without being lonely.

MY STORY: OUR FAVORITE LOCAL RESTAURANT

Once we became empty nesters, my husband and I began to frequent a local restaurant several times a week. Tim was a beloved patron there, and we were friends with the owner and many of the staff. In fact, the week after he died, a place was set in his honor at the end of the bar, with a rose in a vase and his favorite drink poured. This memorial place setting remained there for several days. I know Tim would've laughed at the fact that the bartender was saving his seat for him, even on the busiest nights.

This bar was the place where I hosted the "party" with Tim's ashes in attendance after his funeral service. After several weeks, it took an act of courage for me to return there for dinner one night, alone. To avoid sitting in the dining room alone, I sat at the bar and ordered dinner.

As I waited for my food to arrive, I looked around the restaurant. It was crowded, and I knew several people at the bar.

One friend approached me, but she tilted her head and, with a look of pity, asked, "Oh, how *are* you?" A small group of other friends, all married couples, stopped by, asking the same question, with sorrowful eyes and tilted heads, then moved on to dinner.

But others simply avoided eye contact altogether.

No one joined me at the bar, unlike the old days, when Tim and I sat there and dozens of people would stop by to say hello or sit and chat while we ate.

I quickly realized that bereavement was now stuck on me like the produce sticker on a tomato. I detested the look of pity (and especially the accompanying tilted head), and I was not sure how to respond. I didn't know whether to say, "I'm fine," which was a lie, or "I'm absolutely scared out of my mind," which was true but also a sure way to end conversation. I hated even more the fact that I had no one next to me to talk to— except the bartender. (She was my favorite bartender, but still, she had work to do and I felt like a social misfit.)

Thus, I ate quickly and went home. Walking into my empty house and seeing that urn on the mantel made me want to throw up.

It was a long, long time before I could go back to that restaurant alone.

Do you have a similar story?

HOW TO HANDLE THE SOCIAL WORLD AS A WWPD

As WWPDs, we need our social selves, even if we don't feel very much like socializing. Some very solid research tells us that people who have strong relationships and a sense of community are happier and healthier, even into old age. The Harvard Study of Adult Development (Mineo, 2017) began tracking adult men more than eighty years ago, when they were students at Harvard University. (Back then, in 1938, Harvard admitted men only, so no women were initial participants.) The goal of this study was to answer the question: How can you live long and happy? The current director, Robert Waldinger, tells us the results: Overwhelmingly, the subjects in the study who maintained good, strong relationships lived longer and happier lives.

That's great for men who are Harvard graduates, but is the same true for women—especially those of us who have lost a partner to death and have experienced what is considered to be the most stressful life event one can have?

Researchers Ivana Anusic and Richard Lucas (2013) studied the effects of social relationships and support systems on widows. Interestingly, they found that the relationships women had before they became WWPDs did *not* buffer the pain of widowhood. But it's important to remember that the social networks the WWPD developed prior to the death of her partner *often included her partner.* It makes sense that many of those social networks are not going to be helpful after her partner dies. However, these same researchers reported that women *who developed their own positive relationships* after their partner died adapted to their new life exceptionally well.

And guess what? The sometimes-painful realization is this: It's on you. You are the one who will make a difference in how well your life goes from here on out. All those friends you had before your partner died might remain in your life, and they might not. But that doesn't matter. The one constant in all of this is *you.* The friends that you make, the family members that you seek out, the activities that you participate in are all dependent on you. You're the one in charge.

I love what Krista St-Germain, a widow who is now a life

coach, author, and podcast creator, says: "It was always you." She explains that all the good things that happened to you before your partner died were good because that's how you perceived them to be and that's how you experienced it. Your partner was not responsible for the way you looked at life or how you felt about an experience. *You* were. And that still remains.

Your partner is no longer here, and the people you depended on before might not be so dependable anymore. You alone are the person responsible for your happiness. Sometimes that sucks, because that's a tremendous responsibility when grief hits—as it will continue to do. But it's also kind of liberating to know that you don't have to depend on relationships and social networks that don't assist you in the way that they did before your partner died. You can create your own.

Moreover, the fact remains that we need to be content to be alone, too—because WWPDs are, indeed, alone much more than they were before their loss. Psychologist Ester Buchholz (1997) writes that "being alone gives us the power to self-regulate and adjust our lives" (p. 16). You didn't choose to be alone. But if you can use solitude as a period of self-growth, you might be able to learn to be alone contentedly. You can be alone without being a lonely person. And once you do that, you might also feel a "rebound effect," in which you're able to reconnect with your friends and family and social networks, feeling refreshed and confident.

Ways to Enjoy Being Alone

Part of your ability to find your social persona is to be happy with your solitude. Embrace solitude as a time to become better acquainted with yourself. In the end, the relationship you have with yourself is the most important one. It is, indeed, all about you. Here are some ways to do that.

Spend Time with Mother Nature

How much time do you spend outdoors? According to research, it's time well spent. A recent study that included twenty thousand people showed that those who are outside in natural settings such as parks and beaches for just two hours a week indicated that they have a greater sense of well-being and health than people who stay inside (M. White et al., 2019). Another study indicates that people who took a walk in a natural setting had more positive emotions and less anxiety than those who walked in an urban setting (Bratman et al., 2015). Richard Louv, who coined the phrase "nature deficit disorder," writes that being in nature is a "must-have" for our physical and emotional health (2011).

Whenever and wherever you can, seek the serenity of nature. Go for a walk in the park or neighborhood, bring a plant or two indoors to your living space (and keep it alive!), take a drive to a state or national park. You may be amazed at how much better you feel.

Create a Space You Love

When you get home at the end of the day, do you like being there? Is your home a place where you want to be?

Create a space you love. Paint a room in a soothing, favorite color. Hang artwork or photos that make you smile. Change your drawer handles. Set up an essential-oil diffuser. Fill the space with whatever makes you happy. Include things your partner might never have put in the room. (For example, I remodeled our bedroom and put a white shaggy rug on the floor. I'm certain Tim would never have chosen this rug, but I love it.) Aim to make this space a refuge—a place where, when you go there, you feel lighter, more relaxed, and calmer—so you can actually look forward to going home (even if it is emptier and quieter than it used to be).

Get Yourself Pampered

Get a massage, a manicure, a pedicure, or a new hairstyle. These visits to the hair salon or spa are relaxing, of course, but more importantly they help create a new you—physically and mentally—and prepare you to face the world. (Added bonus: Many nail technicians and hairstylists are wonderful listeners if you feel like talking.)

Hang Up a Sign

Sometimes people want to help too much. They want to fill your days with distractions and lots of company. Having lots of things to do and people to see is good, but you also need some time to be still and think (or be still and not think at all). I love what psychologist Sherrie Bourg Carter wrote in a 2021 article for *Psychology Today*: "A client who owns a community-based magazine puts a sign on her door when she wants alone time. The sign reads 'I'm editing or writing. If the police are here, the office is on fire, or George Clooney calls or stops by, you can interrupt me. If not, please hold all questions until my door opens.'" (The part about George Clooney particularly resonates with me.)

Take Yourself Out to Eat

Dining alone is tough because eating is usually a social thing. However, solo dining has become more popular in recent years. If it's scary for you, but you really miss the lively ambience of a restaurant, take baby steps. Here are some suggestions for going out to eat on your own:

1. Try going to lunch or breakfast first. These are the more casual meals where you're more likely to see solo diners.
2. When you're ready to try dinner, choose your restaurant carefully and make a reservation. Restaurants that have outdoor seating or a bar where you can eat dinner are good choices. A sushi restaurant is a good choice for sitting at a bar area to eat. (Of course, you have to like sushi.)
3. Avoid the busiest dinner times so that the wait-staff is less harried and will pay more attention to you.
4. Dress up a little bit. (Hey, you're going out with your favorite person . . . you!) Looking good for your date with yourself can help you feel more confident.
5. Know where you're going, and think carefully about your transportation. If you want to enjoy a glass of wine or cocktail, of course, drink respon-sibly. Consider taking a cab or Uber or Lyft.
6. Don't be offended by the host or hostess ask-ing, "Just one?" It's not personal, although it can certainly feel that way if you let it. If anything, it's all about the money, so there might be a tiny bit of disappointment in the tone of voice, whether it's intended or not. Restaurants need to make money like any other business, and one diner, of course, doesn't bring in as much as two or more. But stand your ground. No one is really thinking, *That widow should stay home.* You could respond with "Yes, it's JUST ONE. IS MY MONEY GOOD ENOUGH FOR YOU?" But that won't endear you to the waitstaff, who is responsible for putting food in front of you to eat. Instead, you can say,

"I'll be dining alone, thank you," and choose not
to be offended by a statement that wasn't carefully
chosen by someone who really isn't thinking that
much about it anyway.

7. Be sure you're happy with the table they give you.
    Be proactive and ask for a window seat if you want
    one, where people-watching is more likely. Face
    the door if it makes you feel more secure. If the
    host or hostess tries to put you in a corner by the
    bathroom, politely insist on a table somewhere
    else. If that doesn't happen, leave. There are other
    good places to eat that will take your money.

8. Take things to do. Even if you don't use them,
    it might help you to know you have your book,
    e-reader, tablet, phone, or journal with you to
    catch up on some reading, do a puzzle, or write.

9. But try to disengage from your screens as much
    as you can and enjoy your meal, the view, and the
    opportunity to do some people-watching.

10. Take something to save your seat in case you need
    to leave the table during dinner. A scarf, sweater,
    or book will let the waitstaff know you're still
    using the table.

11. Keep your bag secure. Don't hang it on the back of
    your chair, which just asks for trouble.

12. If you become anxious about being alone in a
    restaurant, do some visualizing. What's your
    other option? Picture yourself eating a bowl of
    cereal in your pajamas by the TV tonight. (Is that
    really what you want?) Also remember that the
    world is self-absorbed, and most people really
    do not notice what you're doing there alone.
    Whenever I get a little self-conscious about eating
    out alone, I picture myself being in an airport

restaurant. There, no one cares about noticing me as I eat alone, because they're focused on eating quickly before catching a flight.

13. Consider paying with cash. It makes paying for the bill quicker. And tip well. Letting the waitstaff know that you appreciate them might encourage them to look at solo diners more positively.

14. Keep this in mind: Have you ever noticed couples or families sitting together at a table, glued to their phones, not talking or paying attention to each other? They might be sitting together, but they're definitely not dining together. At least you're not doing that.

15. Promise yourself a reward when you get home. Be proud that you are kicking this widow thing in the ass and becoming a stronger, more resilient, more positive WWPD.

Ways to Enjoy Being with Others

The suggestions below can help you cope with social activities that may have been simple before your partner died but are now challenging.

Break the Awkwardness Ice

You may have noticed that acquaintances who don't know what to say or do around you will go out of their way to remain silent or try to hide. Yet these are people who, nevertheless, you feel connected to and want to chat with. Since chances are they won't make the first move, you'll have to. Besides, this puts you in control of the conversation, and you can steer talk away from awkwardness.

Try to initiate conversation with a story or humorous

personal anecdote. I have broken the ice by telling people some of the nice things that Tim had told me about them or funny stories he had told me that involved them. Here are some examples:

- "Tim often told me the story about the golf outing you took together, and he accidentally overturned the cart."
- "Tim told me many times how much he loved shopping in your store because you carry lots of funny T-shirts. I still have several that he bought for me."
- "Remember the hockey game our boys played in, and Tim had to calm down the screaming moms who were mad at the refs? He often told me how much he loved going to the kids' games, even though some of the hockey moms were crazy."

Immediately, anecdotes like these can eliminate the weird space after "How are you doing?" And it gets people laughing. Everyone feels better after that.

But what about breaking the ice with new people? Even if you find yourself in the position of making conversation with someone you might have nothing in common with, there are still lots of things to talk about. People usually like to talk about themselves, so show interest in them. (It might feel good to talk about somebody else's life for a change. You may even have some wisdom to offer.) Here are some conversation starters:

- What challenges are you facing?
- What's your favorite childhood memory?
- What's your favorite childhood book?

- What kind of music do you like?
- What are you reading these days?

Look Up the App for That

You may have found that one of the worst things about being a WWPD is the isolation you feel now that you're on your own. It might take some real effort to get yourself out of that isolation. Social media and online connections can help. You can find your community with the aid of online platforms such as Meetup. You can enter any interest or hobby you can think of, define your geographical area, and find events or groups that focus on your interest. Meetup is relatively safe because the groups are usually larger numbers of people meeting in public places. You can report abusive users by sending a message to the organizer, who will take actions to remove them. There are meetings and events for just about everything you can think of. I even found an online meeting called "The Healing Power of Humor!"

Social media can be a convenient place to find other WWPDs who share ideas and success stories and in general offer support. Just Google "online support groups for widows" and you'll find a plethora of them. Be sure of these things: (1) The group is well moderated by an administrator, (2) there are current active posts, and (3) the discussion is helpful to you.

Stay away from negativity. Sometimes, given the cloak of the screen and anonymity, people say things that they would not normally say. Be prepared to see some attitudes or outlooks that don't reflect yours about this new WWPD life. That's the beauty of being social even if it is online—you can learn a lot about other people. However, you have no need for judgmental, untruthful, or unkind words. There are lots of scammers and trolls out there, even in groups that are supposedly private and with administrators who are paying attention. If you are subjected to such nonsense, then keep scrolling, delete, block, or remove yourself from the group.

Here are some suggestions for dealing with social media:

1. Schedule your time with social media sites so that you don't get sucked into scrolling endlessly. Plan for no more than an hour a day—maybe a half hour twice a day.
2. If anything bothers you about it, stop. It's just not that important.
3. Disable notifications, because you'll be notified all day long about—well, basically, nothing.
4. If it's too cheerful for you, take a break. Likewise, if it's too sad for you, take a break.
5. Create boundaries. There's no need to overshare. In fact, there's no need to comment or post at all if you don't want to. It's just social media. It's not your life.
6. BEWARE. Protect yourself. Do not give out personal information online. Even a post about going out of town is an advertisement that you are not home and your stuff is free for the taking to someone savvy enough to do so.

Go to the Head of the Class

This might be a great time to learn something you've always wanted to learn, become certified, or get a degree. Think outside the box! For example, one very interesting place to learn something new is the Association for Applied and Therapeutic Humor. This organization has a Humor Research Library, an annual conference, and monthly Zoom meetings. (You can learn and laugh at the same time!) Your local community recreation center or community college might have offerings that would interest you, in subjects from cooking to dog walking to crafting. If you're not up for attending class in person, check out online courses or programs.

Find Your Inner Circle

We know that it's important, especially now that you're a WWPD, to have close relationships with others. In fact, spending quality time with others is vital to your mental health. Seek out your friends who will stick with you, listen to whatever you have to say, and make you laugh. Spend time with them even if you don't feel like laughing.

I'm reminded of when I heard the news that a good friend of mine, Dotty, lost her husband, Allen. A mutual friend, Connie, and I decided to attend the funeral visitation for Allen, who was a local politician and minister in the small town where they lived. I had heard that the visitation was on Friday at a funeral home in that town. We knew there would be lots of people at his visitation. We timed our arrival to be early so we might have a chance to talk with Dotty before she was dealing with hundreds of people offering sympathies. Once we drove up to the parking lot of the funeral home, we were pleasantly surprised to see the lot was empty.

"We beat the crowd!" I exclaimed to Connie. We walked up to the door, which was locked, and slowly figured out that there was nothing going on inside. Googling the funeral home announcement helped me discover, to my dismay, that the visitation was Friday of *next week.* They had scheduled the funeral the week after he died, to give all his family time to make it home. Connie and I decided to call Dotty to tell her what had happened. As a WWPD, I was hesitant, because I was sensitive to the raw, fresh pain that I knew Dotty might be feeling.

But I took the chance and called her. As it happened, Dotty

was so glad to hear from us and graciously invited us to her house. We spent a wonderful hour laughing about the mistake Connie and I made and sharing stories over a glass of wine.

Two years later, Dotty still says that our visit was exactly what she needed that day—just a couple of days after her husband died—laughter and the company of good friends. (The wine also helped a little bit.)

Do you have a friend (or two) who is truly invested in helping you get through this? They're the ones who say, "I don't completely understand what you're going through, but I'd love to listen if you want to talk. And if you want to laugh, I'll help you laugh. If you don't, I'll just be with you."

Lean on those friends. Call them when you need them. Sometimes, even our best friends don't know what to say. Or they may be trying not to bother you too much. If these are friends you really care about, don't be concerned about how often they call. If you want to talk to them, call them. You'll find out very quickly how well they can handle the "new you." If they can't, then simply move on. But don't hesitate to give yourself the opportunity to be cared for by someone who loves you and can help you feel good again.

Just Like Mom Used to Say: Go Outside and Play

As you probably already know, one of the most important things you can do for yourself is to stay physically active. If sports have never been your thing, consider trying something to keep you moving. Besides that, physical activities put you in a social situation where you must interact with other people and make new friends.

For example, you may have heard that pickleball is the fastest-growing sport in America. A 2023 report by the American Pickleball Association states that 19 percent of Americans aged eighteen and over have played pickleball in the last year. There's a reason for that: Anyone who plays it will tell you that it's fun and relatively easy to learn. But most importantly for the WWPD, it's a very social game, with a court that is one-fourth the size of a tennis court. (This size leads to closer proximity to other players, which enables easy conversation.) And, as of 2022, there are 10,724 known places to play in the United States, with 44,094 courts, which means the chances are pretty good that you'll find a place to play (Pickleball Player, 2023).

My friend Sandy, who lost her husband last year, began playing pickleball shortly after he died and now plays ten times a week. In the beginning, one of her new pickleball friends called her daily to remind her to show up at the court and play. Once, her friend just sat with her on the sidelines and let her cry until she was ready to get back in the game. She explained it this way: "Pickleball saved me." Sandy recently told me that she had a colonoscopy one morning, and when she woke up from the anesthesia, asked the doctor if she could play pickleball that afternoon. Her friends have decided that she needs a T-shirt that says, "I Play Pickleball Even After a Colonoscopy." I would argue that pickleball isn't the only thing that saved her—humor did, too.

Playing a game with rules and strategy requires the brain to think of things other than yourself, because you must focus and be in the moment (see Chapter 10). So much suffering comes from the mind reliving the past. Sports and physical activities can help alleviate that pain.

Which of these sports or other physical activities might interest you? Check out your local community center and see if classes are offered or if there are groups you can join.

- Biking tours
- Dancing lessons
- Exercise classes (Jazzercise, Pilates, Zumba)

- Golf
- Hiking tours
- Horseback riding
- Karate
- Kayaking
- Kickboxing
- Marathon running
- Rock climbing
- Rowing
- Skiing
- Swimming
- Tennis
- Yoga

Adopt a Hobby

You've probably already heard "you should find a hobby," as if it's that easy to replace your partner. Of course, it's not that easy. But it's also easy to lose yourself in this transition to your new WWPD life. You've already lost a lot. There's no need to lose more. You might find that learning something new, or rejuvenating what you already know how to do, will refresh your brain just a little bit and help you find a new group of people to spend time with. And it might help you enjoy life a little bit more.

What are some activities you could try? The possibilities are endless, but listed below are a few to ponder—and there's something for every letter of the alphabet! Just like everything else, you can search for these by Googling, checking out your local community center or library website, or looking up a community college for continuing-education classes. Other places to search for new pursuits are retail locations, such as hobby supply stores or wood-crafting shops. Many times, these stores offer classes. And if you're not quite up to getting out, lots of classes are available online and still offer you a chance to be social with other members of the class.

- A—antiquing, auto mechanics classes
- B—baking classes, book clubs
- C—calligraphy, camping (or glamping, as I prefer!) tours, candy-making classes, crafting groups, cooking classes
- D—dog training/walking, drawing lessons
- E—engraving, enameling
- F—face painting, flower-arranging classes
- G—games such as bridge, bunco, chess, pinochle; gardening
- H—home-brewing, houseplants, Hula-Hooping
- I—interior design classes
- J—jewelry-making classes, juggling, jigsaw puzzles
- K—knitting
- L—learning a new language, leather crafting, Lego building
- M—magic, meteorology, miniatures, museum classes
- N—needlework such as knitting, crocheting, cross-stitching, or quilting
- O—opera, origami
- P—painting lessons, photography lessons, poetry-writing classes, pottery classes, puppetry
- Q—quilting, quilling
- R—record collecting, refurbishing furniture, rock painting
- S—scrapbooking, sewing, soapmaking, storytelling, sushi-making classes
- T—travel groups
- U—upcycling, upholstering

- V—video gaming, vintage clothes
- W—wine tasting, writing classes, woodcraft lessons
- X—Xbox gaming, xylophone playing
- Y—yarn crafts, yo-yo tricks
- Z—zip-lining

Go to New Places

You might have favorite places that you frequented with your partner. Those places are special, because they hold memories that you don't share with anyone else. Visit them if you wish. Relish the memories. But also be sure to find new places and events that will help you create your new identity. It doesn't have to be fancy. For example, my husband and I shopped at a local Rite Aid store every Sunday afternoon, using coupons that came out in the morning paper. As silly as it sounds, I've now started shopping at Walgreens. It's closer to home, and its sales are just as good. The change of scenery simply helps me feel a little better about being independent. Additionally, while I still visit our favorite restaurant occasionally when I go out with friends, I've found other spots that I enjoy, with menus that give me new things to try.

Try finding new venues. The change could be refreshing.

Become a Volunteer

Lots of WWPDs go into volunteer work. You probably realize you are much more likely to feel joy when giving to others and when you interact with the people you're helping. Giving your time and talents can make you feel good and forget about yourself for a while. Volunteering for a political campaign or in a social setting such as a hospital, an elementary school, or a recreation center gives you the opportunity to talk to other people and get to know them. In fact, a study done by researchers at Georgia State University (2018) shows that two hours per week of volunteerism reduced loneliness in older adults who have become widowed.

Pick Events in Your Comfort Zone

Some events can be tough if you're going alone. Places that are filled with couples or singles who are trying to become coupled can make you feel lonely, while thinking maybe you should've just stayed home to binge-watch *Yellowstone*.

Since Tim died, I've been to a lot of places and done lots of things, but I still haven't been able to attend a wedding, despite being invited to a couple of them. I just can't do it. Nor do I have to. People will either understand or they won't. And if they don't, too bad. Eventually, I suppose, I'll find the strength to go to one. But I'm comfortable with that for now.

Give yourself some grace. You don't have to attend *everything*. Choose what you can handle right now.

TAKE A DEEP BREATH AND GO

You've experienced one of the toughest challenges life has to offer. You survived, and you're here to tell about it. So reward yourself with the opportunity to see more, do more, feel more, know more. Your sadness is always going to be a part of you, and that can be exhausting. Allow yourself the time to retreat and nurse your grief. But also allow yourself the time to enjoy the company of other people. And most of all, allow yourself the opportunity to enjoy being with yourself.

RESOURCES THAT HELPED ME GET BACK OUT INTO THE SOCIAL WORLD

Cooley, E. (2017). *Newly widowed, now socially awkward: Facing interpersonal challenges after loss.* Atlanta, GA: EL Cooley Publishing.

In this book, psychologist Eileen Cooley offers forty-five essays about her experiences with widowhood, presented in three parts: In the Beginning, After a While, and Over Time. In each essay, Cooley shares her thoughts on the types of social interactions that she endured as a widow. At the end of each essay is a section called "What I Can Do for Myself." Much of the book is somber and, by Cooley's own admittance, sometimes angry in tone. But wry humor shines through an honest treatment of how society treats women who have lost their partners. For example, in "Being Second Choice," Cooley describes the sorrow of waiting for other people to make their social arrangements and fit her in occasionally. She says, "I hope in the future that I learn to appreciate the freedom that being single can bring. I have glimmers of this advantage. Every once in a while I notice that I can be more spontaneous. I can say yes without checking" (p. 97).

Cooley's focus is on the widow's social interactions and feels more like a memoir than a how-to book. Her sections on ways to help herself are based on what she knows as a psychologist, flavored by her personal experiences.

Tidd, C. (2014). *Confessions of a mediocre widow: Or, how I lost my husband and my sanity.* Naperville, IL: Sourcebooks.

Catherine Tidd's delightfully lighthearted memoir makes it clear that there is no one "right" way to grieve or to figure out how to live with widowhood. She tells her story with much self-deprecating humor. While it's not truly a self-help book, it did make me smile and nod my head many times, thinking, Yeah, that's exactly how I feel.

CHAPTER 8

Is This an Episode of *The Office?*

How to Guard Yourself When Going Back to Work

At a moment in which life feels like a maelstrom, work can be a life raft of familiar structure and choice.

—Gianpiero Petriglieri and Sally Maitlis, "When a Colleague Is Grieving" (2019)

If you've recently lost your partner and have decided to go back to work, you might feel, as I did, very displaced. If you work outside the home, you may have found it suddenly difficult to be in the workplace as a WWPD. Do your coworkers stumble over what to say to you? Do they ignore you altogether?

Or maybe you just don't want to return, because it's too painful to be surrounded by people who go on as if life is normal. Lots of WWPDs have difficulty returning to work when expected, because, just like it affects everything else, grief changes the way you think. (Actually, many times widow's fog prevents you from thinking at all!)

I hope this chapter will help you see some of the positive or even humorous sides to going back to work. You'll learn some great tips for things you can do to make working during bereavement a little easier.

MY STORY: BECOMING THAT COWORKER WHOSE HUSBAND DIED

I returned to work after a week of bereavement leave. Basically, I felt as if I had no choice. I was a department chairperson at the university where I also taught two classes. Leaving in the middle of the semester was just out of the question. Besides that, I found the familiar structure of getting up, getting dressed, and solving problems that were not my own was a helpful distraction, and it gave me a sense of purpose.

Yet, sometimes, this "familiar structure" was uncomfortable. It seemed as if my coworkers looked at me differently. There were awkward silences in conversations. I remember one day in particular, a colleague of mine was joking about something she saw on TV with some other faculty members and she blurted out, as people often do, "Oh, I almost had a heart attack when I saw that!" She apologized to me later about saying something insensitive. I appreciated the apology yet felt as if my presence was putting people on edge. My students and advisees sometimes looked lost as they talked with me, because I was supposed to be the one in charge and now I was quite vulnerable.

While most of the time I was glad to be at work, it took every bit of emotional and intellectual energy I possessed to stay focused. Therefore, when a coworker entered my office unannounced, with sorrowful eyes, grabbed my hand, and asked, pityingly, "So, how are you *really* doing?" I felt instantly unnerved. I was annoyed because I had worked very hard to remain focused and her question shattered that focus. And I was immediately suppressing a sob because, well, I was not doing as great as I appeared to be, but I didn't want to sit and cry in the middle of a busy faculty office. It almost seemed as if she *wanted* me to break down and cry.

Because grieving made me sensitive to *everything*, even meetings with colleagues I normally enjoyed working with were sometimes difficult. One day, during a conversation before a meeting began, a couple of my colleagues began good-naturedly complaining about their husbands. In ordinary times, I would laugh and joke right along with them. But, as a WWPD, I had to leave the room. I just could not cope with listening to women complain about their husbands. All I could think was *At least you still have one.*

Thus, while going to work did provide some structure and purpose to my days, it also presented challenges that I did not anticipate.

WHAT CAN HELP WHEN RETURNING TO WORK

You've probably figured out that grief changes your outlook on just about everything. If you enjoyed working prior to becoming a WWPD, you may find that you cannot tolerate the thought of it now. You might have a hard time returning to your career life after your bereavement leave. Even if you return to work willingly and are surrounded by helpful coworkers and bosses, you might find that many things you easily did before are suddenly dreadful chores. Grief comes in unexpected places, times, moments—even at work. And it hits hard, without any boundaries.

Shown below are some suggestions for helping you to cope with returning to the workplace.

Make the Decision: To Go or Not to Go?

If your financial situation is such that you can stay home from work comfortably, then you'll need to make the decision on whether to return. You may find it difficult to leave if your career is a big part of your self-chosen identity. Thus, going back to work might actually become a way to reestablish yourself in your new life as a WWPD.

But before you make any decision at all, find out from your Human Resources Office how much bereavement leave you have available. Whatever it is, if you've decided to stay employed, *take every minute of it.* This is no time to ignore the challenges that face you, so don't be a martyr or kid yourself about how strong you are. (Part of being strong, especially now, is knowing what you need and giving yourself some extra self-care.) You'll probably find that bereavement leave is only enough time to have a funeral and clean up after the guests have left. It's certainly not enough time to come to grips with your new reality and get back to being sort of "normal" again. (There may never be enough time for that!)

If you have the choice to return or not, you could try to ease back into work after your bereavement leave. Set a goal for yourself to try this "working as a WWPD" thing for a month. Then determine how much longer you want to stay on. You might even try working month-to-month to see how well you can handle it. If you hate it after three months and can afford it, then quit. But be sure you've consulted with a financial advisor before you make this long-term decision.

Another way to ease back in is to work half days or fewer days per week. Ask your supervisor or HR manager if this is a possibility, and again, make sure you can handle the resulting loss of income.

Finally, you may want to consider working from home, if that is a possibility. Doing so would give you some flexibility in time and also eliminate the need to commute. But also consider the fact that working from home keeps you from personal contact with other people. While that may seem appealing, it can also be isolating.

Make an Announcement

If you've decided to go back to work, you'll probably find that staying focused on work is prudent—for your productivity as well as your sanity. To stay focused on your work, you will need to let other people know that your partner has died. You cannot assume that everyone knows. Before returning to work, ask someone to let your peers know what has happened, so you don't have to repeat the bad news over and over. Perhaps a single email is all that's needed.

Make Yourself Very Clear

Let your coworkers know how you would like to handle conversations about your spouse.

People may be afraid to talk about your deceased partner because they're afraid it will make you sad or tearful. If you don't mind them talking about your partner and sharing memories, then say so. But if you prefer not to discuss your grief at work, then just politely say that you would like to concentrate on work.

Think about how to convey this information to your colleagues and coworkers. There are some options:

- In the office email that announces your partner's death, include simple instructions about how you would like to handle talking about your partner. Send the email prior to your first day back at work.

- You can send a letter to your Human Resources Department, explaining your wishes, and the HR manager can distribute it.
- Ask a trusted or favorite coworker to spread this message for you.
- Tell coworkers yourself, as you encounter them during your day. After they express their condolences to you, then you can tell them how you would like to handle conversations about your partner.
- Ask someone to arrange a lunch with your coworkers before you return to work. This lunchtime together would be a good place to get all the awkward conversations out of everyone's system, and you can tell them what you're comfortable with going forward.

Be Patient with Yourself

"Widow's brain" is a real condition that surprises a lot of people, especially the WWPD. It's the human body's natural defense mechanism for trauma, creating symptoms such as memory loss, emotional outbursts, and fatigue. Suddenly you may find yourself losing things, having difficulties with tasks that used to be simple, or forgetting dates and times. These conditions certainly do not mix well with your responsibilities on the job, but they are quite natural for the grieving brain and can last a year or more. Thus, it's a good idea to tell your boss and coworkers about the phenomenon, so they don't think you've lost your mind. (Which, actually, you have but just temporarily.)

Listen to Funny Stuff

Sometimes the hardest part of work is getting there—having a silent commute when your mind may fill with thoughts about your partner. Instead, check out humorous podcasts. When you know you're going to have an extended period of silent, reoccurring alone time (like a commute to and from work), fill it with sounds that make you smile. You might find that listening to humor will help put you in a more positive mindset to cope with the pressures of a long workday.

This was especially true on my forty-five-minute drive home from work every day. I discovered that driving alone was much more palatable when I was laughing along with hilarious storytellers or comedians instead of being swallowed up by tension and worry from a difficult day, sad music, or sorrow. Instead, the smiles lingered as I walked through the front door and faced the dreaded empty house.

Here are a few podcasts you could try:

Beach Too Sandy, Water Too Wet—Alex and Christine
    Schiefer, a sibling duo, present dramatic readings
    of one-star reviews written by people who *just*
    need to have their voice heard.
Conan O'Brien Needs a Friend—This weekly podcast
    is about Conan becoming friends with some of
    his weekly guests on his TV show.
Don't Ask Tig—Tig Notaro offers advice on a variety
    of topics, with hilarious results.
Fly on the Wall with Dana Carvey and David Spade—
    Hosts Dana Carvey and David Spade speak with
    fellow alum from *Saturday Night Live.*

The Nateland Podcast—Nate Bargatze talks (and
jokes), along with comedians Brian Bates, Aaron
Weber, and Dusty Slay, about a wide variety of
topics such as fast food, parenting, shoes, and
traveling.

Women Like Us—"Journalists" Jennifer Hudson and
Lillian Bayliss, portrayed by Katy Brand and
Katherine Parkinson, chat about just about anything.

Plan Ahead for Grief Emergencies

Let's face it—it's inevitable that you are going to be interrupted
by your grief. Make a plan for coping with sad moments at
work. If possible, give yourself some daily quiet time for re-
gaining composure. Take a brief break every hour or so. Pull
out your comedy emergency kit, such as a joke, quote, meme,
or comic strip. Let your mind relax from its very difficult work
of trying to cope with grief while it tries to complete your regular work. Figure out a plan for what you will do if a wave of
grief hits during a meeting or an important task. Where will
you go for a minute or two? What kinds of self-talk will help
you keep your composure until the end of the workday? Be as
prepared as possible.

Forgive and Forget

A friend of mine lost her mother. She was terribly disappointed
in her boss because he didn't attend her mother's funeral, and
he seemed distant when she returned to work. This feeling of
being ignored devastated her, and it affected the quality of her
work. She even began looking for another job because she was
so angry at her boss.

Likewise, you will probably encounter coworkers who are

abrupt, aloof, and seemingly uncaring. But keep in mind that you've got enough to worry about without trying to figure out why people don't respond to your grief needs as you would like them to. Sometimes people are simply too wrapped up in their own issues (or the day-to-day grind of work) to care about your grief.

Thus, while it's hard to do, forgive these people. Or at least forget about them or avoid them if you can. You've got enough worries and don't need to be bothered by their insensitivity.

Keep the Door Open to Positive Things

Look for little moments of happiness—or at least moments of distraction. Your brain needs it. My salvation came from the voices of students. My office was right across the hall from a classroom, and if I kept my door open, I could hear the sounds of their laughter from the lively class a colleague was teaching. I also enjoyed listening to students as they walked by my office—many of them peeking in and waving to say hello. These sounds helped me during those tough days when I came back to work after bereavement leave.

Where can you find that kind of brief "happiness distraction" at work? Are there people you work with who would be able to stop and have a cup of coffee or lunch? Can you play cheerful music? Is there something you can hang up or add in your workplace to cheer you—flowers, a photo, a comic strip, or a quote? Search for ways to soothe your working brain, and give it a momentary vacation from grief.

Choose to Do Lunch

As an educator for more than forty years, I have rarely had time for lunch. When I taught in the elementary school, I had about twenty minutes to inhale some food and go to the bathroom.

When I worked at the university, I usually ate a little bit at my desk while preparing lessons or answering emails. But when I returned to work after Tim died, I suddenly felt the need for lunch. I simply had to get away from the noise, responsibility, questions, and tasks that challenged my very tired brain.

This feeling of mine is actually supported in a research study titled "Lunch Breaks Unpacked." In this article, the researchers reported that taking a lunch break and doing something you choose to do is linked with having less fatigue once you get home from the workday (Trougakos et al., 2013).

So I chose to pull away from work, if only for a half hour. My friend and colleague Holly joined me for lunch when she could. We usually just brought lunch from home, but we spread place mats out on a table in my office, put a vase of flowers in the middle, closed the door, and ate our sandwiches and celery sticks. This time gave me a chance to let my brain relax for a few minutes as I ate. Sometimes I ranted to my friend about how much widowing sucked. Other times we told each other funny stories and just laughed. So choosing to pull away from work, if only for a half hour, and chatting with a friend as if we were at a fine restaurant made my whole day better.

Eating a simple bag lunch can be a good break, but you may want to add to that sandwich and make your "get away from work" moments a little more special. Besides getting out of the office altogether and eating out, here are some ideas:

- If possible, get away from your desk and use a separate table. If you cannot do that, remove all your work materials from the table so you have room to eat and relax.
- Bring an LED flameless candle or flowers to decorate your table.
- Bring special plates, cups, and napkins from home to fancy things up a bit.

- Eat your bag lunch outdoors.
- Treat yourself to something out of the vending machine that you normally don't indulge in.
- Put on some soothing and cheerful music.
- Watch a comedy show.

Give Yourself a Break

Take a break when you can; you need it. A meta-analysis of research on the efficacy of microbreaks concludes that short breaks throughout the day are helpful for your well-being (Albulescu et al., 2022). Your breaks don't need to be long; in fact, research also tells us that brief diversions in our focus on tasks can improve that focus (University of Illinois at Urbana–Champaign, 2011). Psychologist and associate professor Mary-Frances O'Connor, who wrote *The Grieving Brain* (2022), explains that grief changes your brain dramatically, because it's working overtime, trying to figure out how to adjust to the absence of your partner.

So give your mind some short little breaks during your workday—a brief break every hour is best. Perhaps these types of breaks will help:

- Have some coffee or tea with a protein snack. (Watch that caffeine, though!)
- Do something that uses a different part of your brain than the part you normally use. For example, if you spend much of the day reading, complete a Sudoku puzzle.
- Do some mind puzzles, such as those on the MindPal app.
- Keep exercise bands in your desk drawer and do some stretches.

- Take a walk.
- Sit outside in the sunshine. (Or sit in the shade if you prefer; just get outside for a few minutes.)
- Read something completely unrelated to work.
- Call a friend or seek out a coworker who can take a brief break with you.

TAKE CARE OF BUSINESS—BUT TAKE CARE OF YOU FIRST

Treat your grieving and working brain kindly. As a WWPD, you've got a lot going on upstairs. Dealing with the work of grief just added to that long list of things you must also manage at work.

If you've decided to return to work while grieving, surround yourself with as much positivity as you can. Look for ways to add humor to your day. Treat yourself kindly, and ask those who work with you to do the same.

Keep your door open to laughter.

RESOURCES THAT HELPED ME AS I GOT BACK TO WORK

Kelly, R. G. (2021). *Taking your griefcase to work*. R. Glenn Kelly Publications.

R. Glenn Kelly, a grieving father whose only child, a son, died in 2013, explains how to handle a "griefcase," which is what we have when we lose a loved one and find ourselves back in the working world. It's "our conscious mind's carrying case that holds all the emotions of our loss" (p. 1). Kelly gives some practical ways to get back to work, positively and productively, while carrying this huge load of anger, confusion, guilt, and pain.

Nawaz, S. (2017, April 28). Returning to work when you're grieving. *Harvard Business Review.* Retrieved from https://hbr.org/2017/04/returning-to-work-when-youre -grieving

The author, Sabina Nawaz, offers some no-nonsense but powerful suggestions for handling grief in the workplace.

CHAPTER 9

Did Cupid Just Shoot Me?

How to Be Open to Finding Love Again

Among those whom I like or admire, I can find no common denominator; but among those whom I love, I can: all of them made me laugh.

—W. H. Auden, "Notes on the Comic," in *The Dyer's Hand and Other Essays* (1989)

Dating again? Does that possibility scare you or create anxiety? What to wear, what to say, where to meet . . . ? Do you feel like a teenager all over again—and not in a good way?

You might be thinking, *What's so humorous or joyful about starting all over with finding love? I already did this once—I don't want to do it again!*

Of all the difficult things you've had to do as a WWPD, dating might be the hardest. As you know, sometimes just getting up in the morning and putting one foot in front of the other can be a challenge. The idea of meeting someone new, having thoughtful conversations (during long walks on the beach, of course), and—yikes!—kissing someone else can be downright frightening.

This chapter seeks to calm those fears and offers new ways to think about the possibility of finding love again.

MY STORY: NOT THE DATING GAME!

Tim and I were married for thirty-eight and a half years. After he was suddenly gone, I had absolutely no intention of dating or falling in love. I spent a year denying that those things were even in the realm of possibility in my life.

But, to put it frankly, I was sick of being sad. And I was bored.

A year after Tim died, I gradually began to grow closer to our longtime friend Robert. We don't live in the same city, so most of our conversations have been via text or phone calls. I discovered that, whenever I talked to Robert, I laughed. When we saw each other, we had such fun. I was starving for fun! His goofiness, lighthearted outlook on life, and love of travel and adventure appealed to me. He also shared my belief in the power of laughter, and in fact, lives that mantra more than anyone I know. He pulled me out of the hole of grief on quite a few occasions.

When one of those bad triggers of grief hits unexpectedly, for no seemingly logical reason, Robert will look at me and say, "Are you having a moment?" And the nice part about that is he doesn't rush to try to cheer me up. He holds my hand and waits until I'm finished. He seems to know that my grief must be validated, honored, and held carefully. Then, when I seem somewhat normal again, he reminds me of something to laugh about—or to at least smile. And when he makes me laugh, I'm reminded of how much sweeter life is when I'm laughing.

I'm fortunate. I found someone who was already a friend and is confident in our relationship, even though I am sometimes a bit of a mess.

A friend of mine recently told me that I am a lucky woman to have found two good men in my life. Remember . . . you were lucky once. You can be lucky again.

WHAT TO DO IF YOU WANT TO LET SOMEONE ELSE IN

So, how can you get lucky? And if not in *that* sense of the word, perhaps you'll be lucky enough to make a new friend or two. Or maybe you'll just enjoy a cup of coffee or glass of wine with a nice new person. Okay, maybe you'll just find out a few interesting things about yourself. Remember, no expectations equals no disappointment!

One thing is for sure: You won't find out anything at all if you don't try. Ready? Here are some suggestions that might help.

Get Back in the Game

I could report on the average number of months a WWPD "waits" to begin dating again. But I won't. (You can Google it if you insist on knowing.)

Why? Because I don't want to even suggest that there is a "right" amount of time to pass before it's "okay" to start dating. (In fact, I don't even like to call this period of time "waiting," because it's as if you are watching the clock and jumping forward as soon as an acceptable amount of time has passed. We both know that grieving consumes too much of your energy to be worrying about a timeline for dating.)

But, at some point, you might feel open to dating again. (And I hesitate to use that word—"dating." It just has so many loaded connotations for a WWPD. Maybe it's best to just think of this activity as "spending a brief time with someone for the purpose of getting to know them.")

Instead of adhering to a superficial timeline, try thinking about how you feel and the stability of your life:

- Are you no longer consumed with grief on a daily basis?
- Are you bored?
- Have your days become more tolerable, with only a few moments of the sharp pain of grief?
- Have you figured out your financial situation, and is it somewhat stable?
- Do you feel like you want someone to talk to about things other than your grief?

If you answer yes to those questions, you might be ready to begin dating again. Maybe things will go well and you'll meet someone delightful and hit it off right away. Or you might find that, at best, you're getting a great education about people that you'd rather not know anything about.

Most important . . . be kind to yourself. If dating doesn't work out for you right away, step back, take a deep breath, and try again later.

Work on Yourself First

Let's face it. While you deserve every sympathetic ear you can find, and you deserve to be sad, you may also be tired of feeling sad all the time. And you may have realized that other people are kind of tired of talking about your sadness, too. (It sucks, I know, but it's a fact: Bereaving people are not always fun to be around.)

It took me about a year (and the amount of time varies for

every WWPD), but I realized that I wanted to be the kind of person others want to be around. In fact, I wanted to be the kind of person *I* want to be around. I finally concluded that I needed some self-love before I could expect anyone else to feel the same way about me. I needed to seek out activities that would help me meet new people and help me focus on things other than myself. Such a focus makes me a stronger, more interesting person.

Thus, I began taking tennis lessons, a sport that I played when I was younger, even though I hadn't held a racquet in years. I plan to start playing golf again, too. (I quit trying to play golf about twenty-five years ago, when my four-year-old son complained about my slow play on the course! It might be time to try again.)

What kinds of activities might you like to try? Hobbies, sports, book clubs, theater, art, music, museums? Getting active can help you make new connections with all kinds of people, but most crucial, it can help you focus on things other than your grief. And that helps you become a person that others enjoy being with.

Dump Your Guilt

You've probably spent some time cleaning out closets, files, or drawers. Have you looked at something that was your partner's and wondered, "Should I get rid of this?" It's a tough decision sometimes. (Hey, I know firsthand. For five years, I've saved the last water bottle that Tim drank from.)

But if there's anything that you *must* toss out, it's guilt.

Remember . . . this is *your* life. Your life doesn't belong to your children, your parents, your friends, your coworkers, your social media network, your church, or anyone else, anywhere, in any capacity. Your life belongs to you. How you respond to the things that happen to you—including the fact that you are now a WWPD—is up to you.

So if you've decided that you're ready to date, or start a new relationship, or just meet someone at Starbucks, it is entirely up to you. Your brain is already too busy trying to overcome the pain of the death of your partner. Don't add guilt to all the hurdles you're already jumping.

And if you're worried that you're going to dishonor your dead partner, stop. You're not. That's a waste of brain energy, so save your energy for something worth worrying about.

Make "Swipe Right" Happen

If you've decided to take the leap into the dating scene—first of all, good for you! This is a big step for a WWPD, and not an easy one. If you're worried that you're not smart enough, or pretty enough, or funny enough, or strong enough, or skinny enough, you can, once again, save your mental energy. What's the worst thing that's ever happened to you? Your partner died, right? That's already happened. So now you can handle this—a mere drop in the bucket.

There are many online dating sites that you can try: Match, eHarmony, EliteSingles, WidowsorWidowers.com, OurTime.com, and Bumble, among others. Many sites are free, with upgrades required for certain features. Look around and get to know their features before you settle on one you like.

If you're going to try online dating, you need to define yourself with your profile. If you're using a site that does not specialize in matches for widows, you will need to decide if you're going to put the word "widow" out there. Like everything else in your new life, it's up to you. Since you probably won't find "WWPD" in a drop-down menu, you'll need to decide between "widow" and "single." Either one works, but there are some things to think about regarding how you will be viewed by others. Unfortunately, some people make assumptions about widows, whether or not they are correct, such as:

- You're wealthy because your spouse left you lots of money. Or you're poor because your spouse left you nothing.
- You're in need of being rescued because your life is in shambles now.
- You've got "baggage"—angry children or stepchildren, lots of grief, feelings of guilt.
- You're ready to have sex on the first date because you haven't had sex in a while. Or you don't want to have sex at all because you think that's cheating on your dead partner.
- You're still stuck on your deceased partner.
- You're sad and no fun at all, just because widows are sad and no fun at all.
- You're angry—well, because life is unfair to widows.

(Isn't it amazing what people assume about a person, based on just one word—without any other information?)

Remember—your profile is not about your past. It's about who you are *now*. You'll want to make a good first impression, and you'll want to put your authentic self forward. Here's an added bonus: Writing a profile helps you learn more about yourself. That's always a good thing.

Here are some tips for creating an online-dating profile:

1. Prepare yourself to write. Make a list of things you want to include. Sit down to write when you're in a good mood and you have time to really think about it.

2. Read other profiles to get an idea of how people present themselves.

3. Write as if you were introducing yourself to a roomful of people, using a friendly, conversational tone, with some humor.

4. Share what you want other people to know. Include preferences and interests, such as your favorite team (if sports are your thing), your ideal vacation (if you like to travel), or your favorite meal to cook (if you like to cook).

5. Whatever you include in your profile will be something you'll talk about with your new date. So be sure it's something you like to talk about!

6. Keep it short.

7. Get a peer review! Ask someone you trust (preferably someone who has tried online dating before) to read your profile for you and suggest any changes. Correct grammatical or spelling errors.

8. Photos don't have to be professionally done, but they should be high quality. Include three to five photos that show you in natural poses, relaxed, and smiling. Your profile photo should be a solo shot. Other photos can include group or activity shots. Include a mix of headshots and full-body pictures. If you have pets that are a big part of your life, be sure to include a photo of you with your pet(s).

9. Use whatever special features the dating site offers, such as videos or audio greetings.

And here are some things to avoid:

1. Do not give your last name or address.

2. Be careful what you make public. Scammers can use details that you've shared to better understand and target you.
3. Stay away from negativity, such as "things I'm NOT looking for," sarcasm, untruths, or exaggerations.
4. No need to list all your degrees or jobs—you're not looking for a business partner.
5. In photos, don't use images that obscure your face, including sunglasses.
6. Avoid selfies. Nothing says "I'm alone and desperate" like a selfie in the bathroom mirror.

Pay Attention to Online-Dating Red Flags

Now that you've put yourself out there and you're receiving messages (yay—someone swiped right!), you need to do your due diligence and become a detective. You've probably heard that online dating is fraught with scammers and people you just don't want to meet. It's sad but true. So protect yourself and look carefully at those profile photos.

Are they proudly holding up a fish on their boat? RED FLAG. Think about it—do you like to fish? No matter how cute they are, if you don't like fishing or spending lots of time in a boat sitting still, this person is not for you. (I got this tip from a friend of mine who learned this lesson the hard way.)

Is their profile picture a selfie taken in front of the bathroom mirror? RED FLAG. Remember what I said about the bathroom-mirror selfie? Enough said.

Do they include photos of them with their late partner? BIG RED FLAG, for obvious reasons.

Does the photo look too—perfect? RED FLAG. It's probably too good to be true, and it might be a scammer, so read on.

Be Careful out There

You've swiped right, your new date swiped right, and it's a match! Now the fun begins. What can you do to protect yourself to ensure a safe and comfortable meeting? Here are some suggestions:

1. Watch for scammers or bots (computer-generated responses). The photos might seem a little too perfect or their messages may feel phony. Research the person's photo and profile by searching online to see if the image, name, or details have been used elsewhere. You can use Social Catfish to find out if someone you've met online is real.
2. Get a second phone number that you use just for dating.
3. Move slowly. Ask lots of questions.
4. Once you've agreed to meet, *you* should pick the place, not your date. Choose a populated place that is comfortable for you, relatively close to home, and easy to leave if necessary, which enables you to be in control of your situation.
5. Use your own transportation.
6. Tell a friend where you're going and with whom. Make an agreement to call that friend if there's a problem.
7. Beware if the person quickly asks you to chat offline. Keep your conversations in the dating site, at least initially.
8. Stay away from a person who claims to love you very quickly, tries to isolate you from friends and family, or asks you for money.

9. If the individual always cancels plans to meet
   with you but continues to communicate with you,
   be suspicious.
10. Google "widow scams." You'll find out more than
    you want to know, but it's smart to pay attention.

Get Away

Over and over again, the WWPDs I have talked to tell me
how refreshing it is to get away from their old environment.
Traveling does, indeed, give you an opportunity to see life differently. Traveling to places you've never been, even outside
your comfort zone, can help you create new memories. And if
you have met someone new, traveling is one sure way to find
out how compatible you are.

You may have heard of the "777 Rule" for a successful relationship. (If you haven't, here it is: Every seven days, go on a
date. Every seven weeks, go on an overnight trip. Every seven
months, go on a vacation.) While that "rule" (and who makes up
dating rules, anyway?) may be a bit unrealistic (and certainly a
little more expensive than many people can afford), there's wisdom in getting to know your partner in all sorts of venues and
situations. You can find out a lot about a person when you eat
in public, sit in snarled traffic, and experience airline delays. It's
good to know these things about your potential partner.

Where can you go? What can you do to step outside the
world that surrounds you right now? Can you take small trips
near your home? Or maybe you can venture farther afield?

Comparing? Stop That!

If you've found someone who interests you, or someone who
turns out to be a new or potential partner—go, you! That's
awesome!

You might be concerned that you're going to compare your date to your late partner. I'll be honest, you probably will. It's really hard not to, especially if you were with your deceased partner for a long time and your relationship was a good, solid one. (And that's a wonderful part of your past that you should be proud of.)

Here's something to keep in mind: You are never going to replace what you lost. As hard as it is to do, it's best to stop trying to compare. (And actually, we tend to overinflate the good qualities of the deceased anyway, making the standards for finding someone new perhaps impossibly high.) Comparing the person you're dating to your dead partner makes two people lose out on what might be a great relationship—or at the very least, a couple of hours of fun: you and your date.

Think of it this way: Have you seen the Mother's Day ads that say, "Be Mom's favorite! Buy her a [fill in the blank with whatever is being sold]"? The reason the ads are (sort of) funny is that everyone knows how Mom doesn't have a favorite— or shouldn't. A mother's capacity to love each of her kids is boundless. She didn't stop loving Child #1 when Child #2 was born—there's plenty of love to go around.

The same is true of the WWPD's new relationship, if one ever develops. You don't stop loving your deceased partner. But because love does not discriminate, you still have room for more love for someone else, if you choose to move into a new relationship.

Here's something else to think about: What *don't* you miss about life with your deceased partner? As you continue on with your new life, perhaps you can surround yourself with more of the things *you* enjoy or hold dear. Your new relationship can be enriched by those experiences.

For example, my husband loved the TV. It was almost always on in our house. I've never watched much TV, mainly because I have severe hearing loss and it's just too much work to pay attention to it. So while he watched TV, I turned off my hearing aids and read a book or the newspaper. It worked for us.

Now, in my new life, the TV is almost never on. Robert and I occasionally watch funny (closed-captioned) YouTube videos together or listen to music (with the volume cranked up). And this works for us.

MOVING ASIDE

You may have heard people say, regarding the loss of someone through death, "It's time to move on." Maybe someone has even said that to you. I contend this statement is a cruel thing to say to anyone who is grieving. "Moving on" implies that the deceased's life was a temporary situation and that the relationship is now part of your past. That's not helpful at all.

Thus, I encourage you, instead of "moving on," to "move aside." Let someone else walk beside you.

Sheryl Sandberg lost her husband suddenly and describes her path to becoming joyful again. In *Option B: Facing Adversity, Building Resilience, and Finding Joy* (2017), Sandberg describes how she learned to "kick the shit out of option B" (p. 13).

While you're kicking the shit out of your option B, try to laugh your way through this new life as much as possible. It might help.

RESOURCES THAT HELPED ME "MOVE ASIDE"

Benedetti, M., & Dempsey, M. (2021). *Finding love after loss: A relationship roadmap for widows.* Lanham, MD: Rowman & Littlefield.

The first two sentences in this book read: "Love is one of the most joyous things that anchors the human experience. That's why it's so hard to give up" (p. 1). The rest of the book is full of practical and compassionate advice about how to begin the "dating" journey again. The book is a comprehensive, guilt-free, user-friendly guide to figuring out new relationships and includes important information about security in online dating; coping with judgment and criticism from friends, family, and other "grief police"; and finances.

Gray, J. (1998). *Mars and Venus starting over: A practical guide for finding love again after a painful breakup, divorce, or the loss of a loved one.* New York: HarperCollins.

As you can see by the title, John Gray wrote from the perspective of any kind of breakup in a relationship; however, he offers lots of sensible advice for women (and men) who have lost a partner to death, without making the mistake of assuming the loss creates the same type of grief. I particularly like Chapter 14, "101 Ways to Heal Our Hearts," which contains suggestions to help you grieve while at the same time bringing positivity to your life. For example, suggestion #60 says, "Remember when you first met; write a letter of gratitude to the person who introduced you and send it."

CHAPTER 10

Grabbing Life by the Bungees

How to Stay Present During Good Times

You're cheating yourself out of today. Today is calling to you, trying to get your attention, but you're stuck on tomorrow, and today trickles away like water down a drain.

—Jerry Spinelli, *Stargirl* (2000)

Maybe you've seen memes or read quotes that say, "Live in the moment." There's even a lively and cheerful song of that title by Jason Mraz. How do you live in the moment? Something tells me that when you became a WWPD, you didn't stop and think to yourself, *Oh, gee, let me get off this grieving train and find a happy moment to live in.*

Grieving for the person you lost and the way of life that is gone consumes you. It's extremely difficult to pay attention to the good moments that surround you, because your brain is so wrapped around your grief.

In this chapter, we'll explore the mantra "Live in the moment." Why is it important? How does it happen for a WWPD? How does it happen for you?

MY STORY: CHARLOTTE AND THE BUNGEE JUMP

A few months after Tim died, I accompanied my daughter-in-law, Sarah, in taking my three-year-old granddaughter, Charlotte, to a festival in Pittsburgh. After eating lunch, we walked over to a small play area for children, where we encountered a bungee trampoline. I had never seen one before, and it fascinated me.

Picture a giant maypole with long metal arms extending from the ground at a sixty-degree angle maybe twenty feet into the sky. Surrounding the maypole were small trampolines, each placed below the extending metal arm, in a circle. Extending from the metal arms was a long bungee cord with a little harness on the bottom of it into which a child could be strapped. Then, once Charlotte started jumping, the combination of the trampoline and the bungee cord created velocity and gravity-defying bounces that made everyone squeal with delight. This experience didn't come cheap. It cost ten dollars for about three minutes.

Charlotte was attracted to it right away and begged her mother to let her try it. Sarah said no, that it was too expensive. That's when I dutifully stepped in as a grandmother, and said, "Oh, she's with Gigi. She can go on." So I paid the ten bucks, and Charlotte was strapped in. We videotaped and snapped photos as she bounced ecstatically, with her eyes lighting up as she soared on each jump. When the three-minute ride was over, as she was unstrapped, Charlotte begged her mom to let her go again. Sarah again said no, that it was too expensive to ride twice and it was time to go home.

Of course, I had to step in again, and said, "Oh, she's with Gigi. Let her go again." Sarah looked at me with a charitable smile (she's such a good daughter-in-law and far more indulgent than I ever was as a daughter-in-law) and allowed the experience to happen twice, in spite of her rules. So Charlotte was strapped in. Once more, she bounced as high as the sky and laughed and squealed. It was a joy to watch—for about two minutes. Then suddenly, she began to wail. In fact, she howled heartbrokenly. We were flabbergasted.

"What's wrong?" we asked. "Does something hurt? Are you okay?"

Finally, between gulping sobs, Charlotte cried, "This ride is almost over, but I don't want to get off! I want to keep riding on it!"

That's when I realized that, sometimes, I'm just like my three-year-old granddaughter: I find it hard to just "live in the moment."

When I'm enjoying a beautiful sunset, or a wonderful time with friends, or a happy holiday occasion, I hear a little teary, nagging voice in my head, saying, "This ride is almost over! I'll go back to my grieving life soon and feel pain again."

As hard as it is to do, I've also realized that it's important to push that chatter in my head aside. Life can change in an instant, as WWPDs know all too well. There's no time to waste. We need to ride out those exhilarating occasions (or maybe just little mundane ones that give us momentary pleasure) until they naturally come to an end—and not end them ourselves prematurely.

And that's what I hope humor and positivity can do for you, too, in the present moment. They can allow you to push aside the pain of grief for a moment, rather than dread the bad moments that might be coming up, even if it's for just a short time.

HOW TO STAY IN THE GOOD MOMENTS

"Enjoy the moment" can be more than just a platitude on a syrupy inspirational-sunrise-photo meme. There are some simple ways to focus on the present and let yourself enjoy momentary happiness when you can find it. Shown below are a few things you can try.

Differentiate "Then" from "Now"

Do you hate it when people refer to your "new normal"? I sure as hell did. I didn't want a new normal. I wanted my old life. I wanted my husband back and the good life that I had with him. But that was then, and this is now. So I had to decide to focus on making my *now* life a good one. It took effort, but this shift in thinking from "then" to "now" gave me a greater sense of agency and control, which provided the strength to power through a lot of tough times. I took so many of the practical yet significant steps I share in this book—all in an effort to help me adjust to my *now* life—and they worked.

Your *then* life may have been utterly fantastic. Honoring that time in healthy ways is good for you, but ruminating on the past can be detrimental if you dwell there for much of your day. Rather than see yourself as having a big, overwhelming, totally *new* life, it may help to position your mind as having a *now* life. So what can you do right *now* to make this moment a positive one? Put down this book and brew a cup of coffee? Message a friend? Paint your fingernails? Pause to watch the birds outside your window? No need to think beyond what's happening right now.

Practice Laughter Yoga

It's hard to live in the moment if the moment isn't a very

pleasant one. So consider Laughter Yoga. Even if you have never done yoga, it's worth a try. This type of yoga is unique because it incorporates laughter that is not preceded by anything funny. In other words, you simply make yourself laugh. Madan Kataria, author of *Laughter Yoga* and founder of the Laughter Yoga movement, explains how laughter is a physiological exercise that improves health and outlook. And the crazy thing about it is you don't need anything funny to laugh at. You don't need jokes or anything humorous to make yourself laugh to reap the benefits. Bringing more laughter into your life can help you shake off those awful trigger moments.

Read Kiddie Lit

Find children's books and read them. They are some of the simplest and best reminders of the importance of seizing the day, of living in the moment, of approaching new things with awe and curiosity. Reread some of your old favorites. If you don't have any old favorites, check out books such as *Hey, Al* by Arthur Yorinks, *The True Story of the 3 Little Pigs* by Jon Scieszka, *Charlotte's Web* by E. B. White, and any of Shel Silverstein's poetry in *Where the Sidewalk Ends*. Remember, it was Dr. Seuss who said, in *One Fish, Two Fish, Red Fish, Blue Fish* (1960), "From there to here, from here to there, funny things are everywhere!" (p. 9).

And if you really want to cheer up instantly, read a book to a child. As Madan Kataria says in *Laughter Yoga* (2018), "Children can teach you how to keep your grown-up mind aside and have fun. You don't have to analyze what is funny and what is not. When you are with children, everything sounds funny" (p. 126).

Channel Your Creative Self

Although I've never been particularly artistically inclined, I decided to learn to paint. I bought some supplies and tuned in to some online tutorials. Surprise! I found out that I could, after all, paint a few things that actually looked good enough to frame and hang. Painting classes took my mind completely off my grief and helped produce a few birthday and Christmas gifts, too. (Of course, my family and friends who are recipients of these paintings might be scratching their heads, trying to find places to put these gifts that they must now cherish.)

There is actually some science behind my artistic self-discovery. Psychology research shows that people who engaged in a creative activity on one day continued to have positive feelings such as enthusiasm and excitement the next day (Conner et al., 2018). Thus, these researchers concluded that doing something creative daily has an impact on overall well-being. These activities help you feel good in the moment but also extend a lingering positive mindset.

What can you create? A painting? A beautiful photo? Something delicious from the kitchen? Artfully refinished furniture? Jewelry? A garden? Poetry? A scrapbook of memories? Any creative endeavor can serve as a new point of reference for your mind and help you focus on something pleasantly removed from grief. And the really good news is the quality of your product is not as important as your ability to enjoy the process of creating it.

Practice Mindfulness Meditation with a Smile

The art of mindfulness has been around for thousands of years, thanks to ancient texts left behind by its founders. It simply means bringing purposeful awareness to the present moment. Meditation is the practice of paying attention. So bringing the two together is about setting aside time to be aware of what is happening right now. The most common mindfulness meditation is to simply pay attention to your breath. This calming, simple exercise is also extremely powerful and can be done in as little as two minutes. But here's a fun twist: Do it with a smile. This brings an extra layer of peace that you did not even know you were craving.

To start, sit or lie down in a comfortable, supportive position where you will not be disturbed for a couple of minutes. Close your eyes and smile (even if you are faking it). Take a slow, deep breath in for the count of four. Pause. Exhale to the count of four. Pause. Repeat this cycle rhythmically and smoothly. If a thought crosses your mind—*I miss my partner, My life is so lonely, This is stupid*—just allow it without getting frustrated and then return your attention to your breath. Stay with the breath, because each breath is your now; your thoughts are the past or future. Return to this mindfulness meditation whenever you are feeling tense, sad, angry, or frustrated. You can do it anytime of the day and in any place whenever you need to feel grounded.

LESSON FROM A THREE-YEAR-OLD

When you find yourself in a "bungee-ride moment," remember that you have the power to control how you perceive any situation. Like my granddaughter experienced, it's easy to prevent yourself from thoroughly enjoying the ride because you dread its conclusion. When you get a joyful moment, stick with it. Enjoy all those bungee rides in life.

RESOURCES THAT HELPED ME STAY IN THE MOMENT

Catignani, E. (2013). *Creative grieving: A hip chick's path from loss to hope.* Austin, TX: Rivergrove.

Elizabeth Catignani writes of her search for ways to cope with the loss of her stillborn son and subsequent death of her husband within a twenty-month period. Her book lists some "creative hip chick ideas" that can help distract you from grief but ultimately help you feel better about yourself, too.

Kataria, M. (2018). *Laughter yoga: Daily practices for health and happiness.* New York: Penguin.

While it's not specifically about dealing with grief, Kataria's book is full of ways to use laughter to maintain emotional balance and "clear the cobwebs of our minds" (p. 141). I have found many of his exercises to be helpful in learning to grab the positive moments and keep them close.

CHAPTER 11

What's the Ripple?

How to Advance Your Partner's Legacy

Ensuring that the good qualities of your loved one will live on in your own life is perhaps the most meaningful of all legacies.

—David Kessler, *Finding Meaning: The Sixth Stage of Grief* (2019)

Sometimes, a WWPD worries that people will forget about her partner once the funeral is over. It's an awful feeling to realize that the person closest to you might now be "out of sight, out of mind" for the rest of the world.

But it doesn't have to be that way. Thinking about how your partner affected this world can be a help in managing your grief, because it gives you purpose and keeps your partner's memory alive.

When you think about your partner, what sticks out in your mind?

What did your partner mean to other people?

What words would other people use to describe your partner?

What is your partner's legacy?

What did you love most about your partner? How can you "be" that?

This chapter is about finding meaning in your grief. Let's focus on discovering ways to help your partner's memory live on, and in so doing, transform the pain of your grief into something positive.

MY STORY: TIM'S GENEROSITY LIVES ON

My husband was lots of things—generous, full of advice, grateful, stubborn, polite, responsible, and funny. Thus, I try to take on some of those qualities as well. (Well, I don't have to *try* to be stubborn. That comes naturally.)

On one of our very first dates, way back in 1978, before we were married, we went to a restaurant in St. Petersburg, Florida, for dinner. Tim paid for it, and in those days, he could barely afford luxuries such as eating out. He calculated how much we could spend on dinner so that he had money to tip the waiter 25 percent. At the young age of twenty-one, with very little money in his own pocket, he thought about tipping the waiter *first*, before we ordered our food. And he told me, "That's just the right thing to do."

Tim's generosity toward people who helped him, in any capacity, was legendary. My husband truly believed that a measure of a person's worth was in how you treat people who work for you. And his generosity extended beyond his wallet. He also spent time talking to waiters, waitresses, bartenders, luggage handlers, retail salespeople, delivery people, mail carriers, and housekeeping staff wherever he went. He was genuinely interested in other people's lives and was always ready to tell a story or offer life advice.

That may be why, at the end of the very long day of Tim's funeral visitation, I looked up to see the very last person in line. It was Larry, a curbside baggage handler at Pittsburgh International Airport. We often saw Larry when we traveled, and Tim always took the time to stop and talk to him (even when we were in a hurry to catch a flight). So, on the day of the visitation, Larry rushed over to the funeral home after work and stood in that long line, still in his uniform, to pay his last respects to a man who was generous with his money and his heart.

WHAT LIVES ON FOR YOU?

American psychiatrist Irvin Yalom (2008, p. 8) describes the "ripple effect" in an article he wrote about death anxiety. He says, "Rippling refers to the fact that each of us creates—often without our conscious intent or knowledge—concentric circles of influence that may affect others for years, even generations." It was enormously helpful for me to remember the effect that Tim had on other people.

What are some ways you can experience your partner's ripple effect?

Savor Ongoing Connections

Psychologist Lucy Hone (2017) calls the tangible items that help the bereaved feel closer to the departed "ongoing connections" (p. 197). It took me a year to throw away Tim's toothbrush. But five years later, I still have lots of ongoing connections that make me smile, such as a very ugly and frightening-looking Christmas nutcracker that our daughter-in-law gave him as a joke, his work ties, a miniature golf cart to remind me of the time he crashed a real one, and a miniature box of Froot Loops to remind me of Tim's favorite cereal.

My most important ongoing connection, however, is what I believe to be the last thing he touched: his water bottle. Tim must've taken about four or five sips from that bottle before going to bed, and it has been on the nightstand since the early morning of February 16, 2018.

About a year ago I had the bedroom repainted while I was out of town. When I returned, I was delighted with the new color of the room but stricken with agony when I realized the water bottle was missing. I frantically called my painter, asking the seemingly illogical question, "Do you know where that half-empty water bottle on the bedside table might be?"

Luckily, he hadn't thrown it away, and he didn't ask any questions about why I might be saving it. He had placed it on a shelf in the laundry room, along with some other items he moved out of the way.

So I returned Tim's water bottle to its spot on the table. It is not going anywhere, at least for now. And I'm pretty sure my very practical husband would find it enormously funny that I've saved a half bottle of water for more than five years.

I have not been able to part with these things. Thus, I urge you to keep whatever you want to keep. Logic doesn't matter. It's your way of remaining connected to your partner, and there's absolutely nothing wrong with that.

Write Letters

On Tim's birthday and on the anniversary of his death each year, I write a letter to each of my sons and my grandchildren. In these letters I tell them stories about things Tim did and how I see those stories reflected in their personalities and their current lives.

For example, I wrote to my oldest son, Chuck, how our family trip to see the Fourth of July fireworks showed me how very much he is like his father. As the end of the show became apparent, Chuck scrambled around and rushed all of us to the car so we could beat the traffic. It reminded me of the fact that never, in all the years I knew my husband, did we attend any sporting event all the way to its conclusion. Why? Because Tim wanted to beat the traffic. He always said it was just the most efficient thing to do, and besides, we could listen to the rest of the game on the radio as we drove home. Ah, Chuck has turned out to be so much like his father, and I hope he's proud of that. I know I am.

What can you write in a letter to honor your partner's memory? Send it to someone who would love to hear these words. Or, if you prefer, try writing the letter but then putting it away to read later.

Establish a Way to Pay It Forward

What was your partner known for? What were some of their hobbies or passions? Seek out opportunities to honor your partner by contributing time or resources to organizations that are associated with their passions. Many people ask for donations to charitable organizations in memory of their deceased partner, in lieu of flowers at the funeral. But you might find that more personal involvement makes you feel good and gives you a sense of purpose that you might not have had before your partner died. Maybe you can volunteer an hour or two per month, or organize a charitable collection, or participate in a walkathon.

My son Tommy is a professional golfer, and his dad was enormously proud of that. Before Tommy was born, Tim played golf frequently, usually in charity outings. He was not a great golfer, but he played to raise money for various organizations or develop his business networks. Once Tommy came around to the sport and began playing golf at a very young age, Tim quit playing. He began following his son on junior tours. He often said, when explaining why he quit playing, "I now know what good golf looks like, and I don't want to spend time playing bad golf. I'd rather watch my son play good golf."

Thus, my sons have organized an invitational professional golf tournament in their father's memory that raises money for Tim's favorite charities. This event has become a highlight of the year for our family. We thoroughly enjoy the opportunity to listen to and tell humorous stories about Tim, while raising money for charitable causes that were dear to him. And I hope that Tommy takes his dad's words with him to the course every time he plays.

Lights, Camera, Action! Put Those Old Photos and Videos to Use

Have you been cleaning out closets and drawers? Did you find any old photos or videotapes? Perhaps you can pull together some images to create a new personal video to share with others. This recording would be a wonderful way to help keep your partner's memory alive for your family and friends.

A friend of mine who became a WWPD decided that her late husband's old family photos were so interesting that she decided to use her time and energy to research his family history. She's recorded it in a self-published book that she's shared with her children and grandchildren. She says they have thoroughly enjoyed the personal stories she's told over the years.

Another idea is to put together a simple self-published photo book with some captions that tell your partner's life story. This idea is relatively simple and inexpensive to do. Many photo services have templates that enable you to create the book without any skills in graphic design needed.

Borrow a Tradition

Honoring the dead in American culture is usually done with sadness in a somber manner, but maybe you'd like to do something a little more lighthearted. Perhaps you could borrow some ideas from other cultures. Consider these:

- In the African country of Ghana, people in some communities make "fantasy coffins" for burying their loved ones. These coffins are made to reflect the life and profession of the person who died. For example, a truck driver may have a coffin shaped like a truck. Or families produce coffins that depict animals based on the personality of the deceased, such as a lion for someone who was a strong leader. Similarly, people in Bali who believe in reincarnation have the Ngaben celebration, where they create a casket shaped like an animal for the ashes of the deceased. It may be too late for you to have a coffin made. But if you're reading this book after your partner's cremation and have wondered what to do with the ashes, you could consider having a small coffin made like the fantasy coffins in Ghana.
- In Japan, people honor their dead with the Obon festival, which is a Buddhist celebration. During the three-day festival, families tidy up their ancestors' graves. They attend carnivals, enjoy festival foods, and participate in traditional dances to the sound of *taiko* drums. In likewise fashion, perhaps you can invite family and friends to a celebratory dinner filled with foods and music that your partner loved.
- Right here in the United States, in New Orleans,

some people celebrate the life of a loved one with the "second line," or a jazz funeral. Family and friends of the deceased line up at the funeral home in a somber procession. But after the ceremony is over, the music changes and the procession marches through town to lively jazz music. If your partner loved jazz, why not host a celebration with a jazz band or a DJ that plays jazz? Or celebrate with whatever kind of music your partner loved.

THE RIPPLE EFFECT

The ripple effect is quite powerful. It's how your partner is remembered as their memory lives on in your life and the lives of others. It can make you smile as you remember good times and funny stories. It can make the world a better place.

Let the ripple effect strengthen you.

RESOURCES THAT HELPED ME FIGURE OUT HOW TO INCREASE THE RIPPLE EFFECT

Hone, L. (2017). *Resilient grieving: Finding strength and embracing life after a loss that changes everything.* New York: The Experiment.

While Hone doesn't speak from the perspective of the widow, she certainly knows deep grief and shows the reader how to figure out their "brave new world" (p. 173). My copy of the book is filled with notes in the margins where I had a-ha moments and gained so much insight about how to weather this thing called grief. She made me realize that it's okay to not give all Tim's stuff away and to hang on to whatever gave me comfort. She also showed me that resilience is all about making choices in the way we grieve. Hers is a powerful book.

Kessler, D. (2019). *Finding meaning: The sixth stage of grief.*
New York: Scribner.

In this book, David Kessler, coauthor of On Grief and Grieving, *pur-
ports that once acceptance is realized, the person who has experienced
loss can search for meaning in their loved one's death. Kessler's book is
about making that meaning a reality. His writing is honest, profound,
and tender, coming from a place of knowledge in an academic sense
as well as being deeply personal. He wrote the book after losing his son
David to an accidental drug overdose. Although written for anyone
who is grieving, this book can help the widow manage her grief in ways
that improve her life and the lives of others. As Kessler says, "all of us
get broken in some way. What matters is how we get up and put the
pieces back together again" (p. 28).*

Epilogue

One night, Tim and I were eating dinner at our favorite local restaurant. It was crowded, but we managed to find a seat at the bar. One of our favorite bartenders, Tracy, was at work, and we chatted with her for a while. I ordered the salmon with chopped salad, as usual, while he had his favorite, the tomato vodka pasta with chicken. (Yes, I still remember what we ordered!) Because a friend of the family had recently died, we got on the subject of death and funerals. (Yes, I know. We were such lively conversationalists.) As we finished our meal, Tim looked at me with a completely straight face and said, "When I die, you get a proper mourning period of about a week. Then go live your life. Have fun."

I snorted in my wine. But then, without hesitation and with an equally straight face, I said, "Sure. No problem!"

Of course, after it actually happened, I realized that he had no earthly idea what he was talking about. It was physically, emotionally, and humanly impossible for me to have a "proper mourning period of about a week."

But I've since realized that he gave me the best gift anyone could ever give a grieving spouse: a plan to carry on with a smile. (I think he would have enjoyed that bungee ride immensely. He hated roller coasters, but he managed to ride on one with our son Tommy numerous times. I think he would've somehow figured out how to join his granddaughter Charlotte on her bungee ride.)

Even though his death was sudden and unexpected, I had a

very good idea of how to take care of things, because he shared his wishes with me many times. Those wishes included an expectation to laugh and have fun. I hope to continue doing that for all my remaining days. Thanks, Tim, from the bottom of my heart. I'm forever grateful.

Acknowledgments

This is the book I never wanted to write. But now I'm so glad I did. And it takes great effort to make mere words on a screen become a published work. That effort cannot be made alone. I have so many people to thank.

Way back in the beginning, when the manuscript was just a collection of thoughts, I consulted Kimberly Meilun, a developmental editor. Thank you, Kimberly, for helping me shape those initial thoughts into something my audience might want to read.

As the manuscript moved through its next stages and became something that might be recognizable as a book, I was lucky enough to get support and help from Marisa Solis, a developmental editor and book coach but also a darn good cheerleader. Marisa, thank you for providing me with your wisdom and unflinching feedback and also for believing in me and the worth of this book. It wouldn't be what it is without you.

The production team at Girl Friday Productions has been supportive, professional, and knowledgeable. I'm lucky to have been able to work with a team who guided me patiently and expertly. Thank you to Adria Batt, Janice Lee, Paul Barrett, Abi Pollokoff, and Jaye Whitney Debber for dedicating yourselves to this book. I'm so grateful for your expertise, your help, and your positivity. Sara Addicott, my senior publishing manager, you've stuck with me every step of the way, answering a multitude of questions, forgiving me for missed meetings or forgotten tasks, and coordinating all the moving parts of this production. And besides that, you've been just plain fun to talk to. Thank you.

Thank you to my WWPD friends: Connie Armitage, Dotty Campbell, Midge Kennedy, Toy Martinez, Sandy McWilliams, Bev Roseen, and Jane Wells. I'm so sorry that you've had to travel this road, but I'm glad we've been able to share some laughs along the way. Thank you for feedback, suggestions, and inspiration for various parts of this book.

Thank you to my friend Ginny Hannan for your support during my most difficult time. You just showed up, and I'll always be grateful.

Thank you to my friend and favorite neighbor Kathy Russo for knowing just what to do, as always.

Thank you to my friend and colleague Holly Diehl. I don't know what I would have done without you. You listened. You never relied on platitudes. And you helped me keep my head on straight.

Thank you to my friend Trish Macartie for helping me make my home a place that I love again, something I recommend enthusiastically for all WWPDs.

To David Russo, thanks for patiently answering a multitude of questions about stuff I never wanted to deal with, offering advice only when asked, and making practical suggestions for this book.

Thank you to my sisters, Tricia Harrison and Annie Eller, for being what sisters should be and for helping me find the funny side of just about anything.

To my mother, Marilyn Hood, thank you for making me feel like a star every time I walk into the room—even now. And to my father, Bob Hood, thank you for instilling in me a love of language and a sense of humor from the beginning.

To the women in my sons' lives, I thank you for being the daughters I never had. Sarah, you held a special place in Tim's heart. Thank you for giving him so many smiles, for unfailingly supporting me as I wrote this book, and for providing Chuck with the support he needed at a difficult time. Crystal, thank you for being so supportive of Tommy and for not being afraid to learn about Tim through our family folklore.

Thank you to my three grandchildren, Charlotte, Abigail, and Nicklaus, for helping me to keep Pap-Pap's memory alive by listening to my stories about him and for inspiring so many parts of this book.

To Robert, I thank you for always making me laugh.

And finally, but most importantly, thank you to my sons. Chuck, you had to travel this road way too soon, and yet you've done it with strength, grace, and positivity. Tommy, you've faithfully followed all the paths your father laid out for you, and then found the strength to walk your own. You also found strength to occasionally say, "Hey, Mom, we need to talk." Both of you have been unwavering in your support of your sometimes clueless mother. You've given me so many reasons to smile.

References

Aikman, B. (2013). *Saturday night widows: The adventures of six friends remaking their lives.* New York: Broadway Books.

Albom, M. (2013). *The first phone call from heaven.* New York: HarperCollins.

Albom, M. (2012). *The time keeper.* New York: Hyperion.

Albulescu, P., Macsinga, I., Rusu, A., Sulea, C., Bodnaru, A., & Tulbure, B. (2022, Aug. 31). "Give me a break!" A systematic review and meta-analysis on the efficacy of micro-breaks for increasing well-being and performance. *PLOS One.* doi: 10.1371/journal.pone.0272460.eCollection 2022

Anusic, I., & Lucas, R. (2013). Do social relationships buffer the effects of widowhood? A prospective study of the adaptation to the loss of a spouse. *Journal of Personality, 82*(5), 367–378.

Armstrong, A., & Donahue, M. (2012). *On your own: A widow's passage to emotional and financial well-being* (5th ed.). Washington, DC: On Your Own Publishing Company, LLC.

Auden, W. H. (1989). Notes on the comic. In W. H. Auden, *The dyer's hand and other essays* (pp. 371–385). New York: Vintage International.

Barry, D. (2012). *Dave Barry's book of bad songs.* Kansas City, MO: Andrews McMeel Publishing.

Barry, D. (2006). *The shepherd, the angel, and Walter the Christmas miracle dog.* New York: Penguin/Berkley Publishing.

Benedetti, M., & Dempsey, M. (2021). *Finding love after*

loss: A relationship roadmap for widows. Lanham, MD: Rowman & Littlefield.

Bennett, R. (2011, June 30). The TGB interview: Betty White. *Time Goes By.* Retrieved from https://www.timegoesby .net/weblog/2011/06/the-tgb-interview-betty-white.html

Bonanno, G. (2019). *The other side of sadness: What the new science of bereavement tells us about life after loss.* New York: Basic Books.

Bratman, G., Daily, G., Levy, B., & Gross, J. (2015). The benefits of nature experience: Improved affect and cognition. *Landscape and Urban Planning, 138,* 41–50.

Buchholz, E. (1997). *The call of solitude: Alonetime in a world of attachment.* New York: Simon & Schuster.

Cambridge Dictionary. (n.d.). Positivity. In *Cambridge dictionary.* Retrieved November 11, 2023, from https:// dictionary.cambridge.org/dictionary/english/positivity

Carter, S. (2021, Jan. 31). Six reasons you should spend more time alone. Available from https://www.psychologytoday .com/us/blog/high-octane-women/201201/6-reasons -you-should-spend-more-time-alone

Catignani, E. (2013). *Creative grieving: A hip chick's path from loss to hope.* Austin, TX: Rivergrove.

Compton, J., & Pollak, R. (2021, May 14). The life expectancy of older couples and surviving spouses. *PLOS One, 16*(5). doi: 10.1371/journal.pone.0250564

Conner, T., DeYoung, C., & Silvia, P. (2018, Nov. 17). Everyday creative activity as a path to flourishing. *The Journal of Positive Psychology, 13*(2), 181–189. doi: 10.1080/17439760.2016.1257049

Cooley, E. (2017). *Newly widowed, now socially awkward: Facing interpersonal challenges after loss.* Atlanta, GA: EL Cooley Publishing.

Devine, M. (2017). *It's OK that you're not OK: Meeting grief and loss in a culture that doesn't understand.* Boulder, CO: Sounds True.

Fey, T. (2011). *Bossypants.* Boston: Back Bay Books.

Frederickson, B. (2009). *Positivity: Discover the upward spiral that will change your life.* New York: Harmony Books.

Fulghum, R. (2003). *All I really need to know I learned in kindergarten: Uncommon thoughts on common things* (25th anniversary ed.). New York: Ballantine.

Gaffigan, J. (2014). *Dad is fat.* New York: Crown Archetype.

Georgia State University. (2018, April 16). Volunteering 2 hours per week reduces loneliness in widowed older adults. *ScienceDaily.* Retrieved June 11, 2023, from www .sciencedaily.com/releases/2018/04/180416185559.htm

Gray, J. (1998). *Mars and Venus starting over: A practical guide for finding love again after a painful breakup, divorce, or the loss of a loved one.* New York: HarperCollins.

Grisham, J. (2010). *Skipping Christmas.* New York: Anchor.

Haley, E. (2021). After a death, the holidays are a secondary loss. Retrieved from https://whatsyourgrief.com/after-a -death-the-holidays-are-a-secondary-loss/

Haley, E. (2014). New perspective on old traditions: Grief and the holidays. Retrieved from https://whatsyourgrief.com /grief-and-the-holidays/

Holiday, R. (2014). *The obstacle is the way: The timeless art of turning trials into triumph.* New York: Penguin.

Holmes, T., & Rahe, R. (1967). The social readjustment rating scale. *Journal of Psychosomatic Research, 11*(2), 213–218.

Hone, L. (2017). *Resilient grieving: Finding strength and embracing life after a loss that changes everything.* New York: The Experiment.

Josephs, R. (1954, September 5). Robert Frost's secret. In *The Cincinnati Enquirer: This Week Magazine, 2,* Column 1.

Kataria, M. (2018). *Laughter yoga: Daily practices for health and happiness.* New York: Penguin.

Keillor, G. (2011). *A Christmas blizzard.* New York: Penguin.

Kelly, R. G. (2021). *Taking your griefcase to work.* R. Glenn Kelly Publications.

Keltner, D., & Bonanno, G. A. (1997). A study of laughter and dissociation: Distinct correlates of laughter and smiling during bereavement. *Journal of Personality and Social Psychology, 73*(4), 687–702.

Kesey, K. (1962). *One flew over the cuckoo's nest.* New York: Signet.

Kessler, D. (2019). *Finding meaning: The sixth stage of grief.* New York: Scribner.

Kilmartin, L. (2018). *Dead people suck.* New York: Rodale.

King, B. (2016). *The laughing cure: Emotional and physical healing—A comedian reveals why laughter really is the best medicine.* New York: Skyhorse Publishing.

Klein, A. (1989). *The healing power of humor: Techniques for getting through loss, setbacks, upsets, disappointments, difficulties, trials, tribulations, and all that not-so-funny stuff.* New York: Jeremy P. Tarcher / Putnam.

Klein, A. (1998). *The courage to laugh: Humor, hope, and healing in the face of death and dying.* New York: Jeremy P. Tarcher / Putnam.

Kross, E. (2021). *Chatter: The voice in our head, why it matters, and how to harness it.* New York: Crown.

Kübler-Ross, E., & Kessler, D. (2005). *On grief and grieving: Finding the meaning of grief through the five stages of loss.* New York: Scribner.

Lamb, W. (1994). *Wishin' and hopin'.* New York: Harper.

Lazear, J., & Lazear, W. (1993). Erma Bombeck quote. In *Meditations for parents who do too much.* New York: Fireside/Parkside.

Louv, R. (2011). *The nature principle: Reconnecting with life in a virtual age.* Chapel Hill, NC: Algonquin Books.

MacLeod, C., Rutherford, E., Campbell, L., Ebsworthy, G., & Holker, L. (2002). Selective attention and emotional vulnerability: Assessing the causal basis of their association through the experimental manipulation of attentional bias. *Journal of Abnormal Psychology, 111*(1), 107.

McInerny, N. (2019). *The hot young widows club: Lessons on survival from the front lines of grief.* New York: TED Books / Simon & Schuster.

Meekhoff, K., & Windell, J. (2015). *A widow's guide to healing: Gentle support and advice for the first five years.* Naperville, IL: Sourcebooks.

Mineo, L. (2017, April 11). Good genes are nice, but joy is better. Available from https://news.harvard.edu/gazette /story/2017/04/over-nearly-80-years-harvard-study-has -been-showing-how-to-live-a-healthy-and-happy-life/

Mork, M. (2019). *Navigating grief with humor.* Coppell, TX: Kindle Direct Publishing.

Nawaz, S. (2017, April 28). Returning to work when you're grieving. *Harvard Business Review.* Retrieved from https://hbr.org/2017/04/returning-to-work-when-youre -grieving

News Direct. (2023, March 29). New APP research reveals nearly 50 million adult Americans have played pickleball in the last 12 months. Retrieved from https://newsdirect .com/news/new-app-research-reveals-nearly-50-million -adult-americans-have-played-pickleball-in-the-last-12 -months-average-age-drops-to-35-187943348#:~:text =The%20latest%20research%20reveals%20that,are%20 between%202018%20and%202024

O'Connor, M. (2022). *The grieving brain.* New York: Harper One.

Oxford Languages. (n.d.). Positivity. In *Google's English dictionary*. Retrieved November 11, 2023, from https://www.google.com/search?q=positivity+definition&oq=positivity+definition&aqs=chrome..69i57j0i512l2j0i22i30l3j0i10i22i30j0i22i30l3.5114j1j7&sourceid=chrome&ie=UTF-8

Petriglieri, G., & Maitlis, S. (2019, July–August). When a colleague is grieving: How to provide the right kind of support. *Harvard Business Review, 97*(4), 116–123.

Pickleball Player. (2023, March 17). Pickleball popularity statistics and demographics: Facts and infographic. Retrieved from https://thepickleballplayer.com/pickleball-popularity-statistics-demographics-infographic/

Provine, R. (2000, Nov. 1). The science of laughter. *Psychology Today*. Available from https://www.psychologytoday.com/us/articles/200011/the-science-laughter

Reynolds, D., & Hannaway, D. (2015). *Make 'em laugh: Short-term memories of longtime friends*. New York: William Morrow.

Rowe, M. (2019). *The way I heard it*. New York: Gallery Books.

Sandberg, S., & Grant, A. (2017). *Option B: Facing adversity, building resilience, and finding joy*. New York: Alfred Knopf.

Schwalbe, W. (2012). *The end of your life book club*. New York: Knopf Doubleday.

Scieszka, J. (1989). *The true story of the 3 little pigs*. New York: Viking Penguin.

Seuss, Dr. (1960). *One fish, two fish, red fish, blue fish*. New York: Random House.

Silverstein, S. (1974). *Where the sidewalk ends*. New York: HarperCollins.

Sincero, J. (2013). *You are a badass: How to stop doubting your greatness and start living an awesome life.* Philadelphia, PA: Running Press Book Publishers.

Smith, E. (2021, December 31). How to develop a positive personality. *HealthyPlace.* Available from https://www .healthyplace.com/self-help/positivity/how-to-develop -a-positive-personality

Spinelli, J. (2000). *Stargirl.* New York: Alfred Knopf.

St-Germain, K. (2023). *The widowed mom podcast.* Available from https://www.coachingwithkrista.com /podcastlaunch/

Stifter, K. (2020). *The funny thing about grief.* Saint Paul, MN: Beaver's Pond Press.

Strack, F., Martin, L., & Stepper, S. (1988). Inhibiting and facilitating conditions of the human smile: A non-obtrusive test of the facial feedback hypothesis. *Journal of Personality and Social Psychology, 54*(5), 768–777.

Streeter, L. G. (2020). *Black widow: A sad-funny journey through grief for people who normally avoid books with words like "journey" in the title.* New York: Little Brown & Co.

Thompson, B. L. (2020). *Sudden widow: The story of love, grief, and recovery, and how badly it can suck!* New York: Brooklyn Writers Press.

Tidd, C. (2014). *Confessions of a mediocre widow: Or, how I lost my husband and my sanity.* Naperville, IL: Sourcebooks.

Trougakos, J., Hideg, I., Cheng, B., & Beal, D. (2013, March 25). Lunch breaks unpacked: The role of autonomy as a moderator of recovery during lunch. *Academy of Management Journal, 57*(2), https://doi.org/10.5465 /amj.2011.1072

University of Illinois at Urbana–Champaign. (2011, February 8). Brief diversions vastly improve focus, researchers find.

ScienceDaily. Retrieved from www.sciencedaily.com /releases/2011/02/110208131529.htm

US Census. (2021). Selected social characteristics in the United States: American community survey data. Retrieved from https://data.census.gov/table?q=dp02 &tid=ACSDP1Y2021.DP02

Wadlinger, H. A., & Isaacowitz, D. M. (2008). Looking happy: The experimental manipulation of a positive visual attention bias. *Emotion, 8*(1), 121.

Weems, S. (2014). *Ha! The science of when we laugh and why*. New York: Basic Books.

What's Your Grief. (2023). What's your grief. Retrieved from https://whatsyourgrief.com

White, B. (1987). *Betty White: In person*. New York: Doubleday.

White, E. B. (1952). *Charlotte's web*. New York: HarperCollins.

White, M., Alcock, I., Grellier, J., Wheeler, B., Hartig, T., Warber, S., Bone, A., Depledge, M., & Fleming, L. (2019). Spending at least 120 minutes a week in nature is associated with good health and wellbeing. *Scientific Reports, 9*(7730). https://doi.org/10.1038/s41598-019-44097-3

Yalom, I. (2008). The ripple effect. *Therapy Today, 19*(4), 6–11. https://www.bacp.co.uk/bacp-journals/therapy -today/may-2008/the-ripple-effect/

Yorinks, A. (1986). *Hey, Al*. New York: Farrar, Straus & Giroux.

Zander-Schellenberg, E., Collins, I. E., Miché, M., Guttman, C., Lieb, R., & Wahl, K. (2020). Does laughing have a stress-buffering effect in daily life? An intensive longitudinal study. *PLOS One, 15*(7). Available from https://doi .org/10.1371/journal.pone.0235851

About the Author

Photo © Mark J. Media 2023

Dr. Diane H. Nettles began her career teaching grades K–4. After earning her doctorate in curriculum and instruction, she taught for one year at Gallaudet University, then moved to the Pittsburgh area, where she was a faculty member and chair of the Childhood Education Department at Pennsylvania Western University in California, Pennsylvania. In her thirty-two years at the university, she won numerous faculty and teaching awards. In the five years since her husband passed away, she has devoted her energies to discovering and researching the value of humor and positivity to meet life's biggest challenges. When she's not writing, her favorite pastimes include gardening, traveling to all the places in this world she and her husband wanted to see, playing pickleball, learning how to paint, and making valiant attempts to play tennis. Through it all, she works diligently to avoid the "w" word— "widow"—and to live her new life skillfully.